# Perception : Facts and Theories

*C. W. K. MUNDLE*

# Perception: Facts and Theories

OXFORD UNIVERSITY PRESS
*London Oxford New York*
1971

*Oxford University Press*
OXFORD LONDON NEW YORK
GLASGOW TORONTO MELBOURNE WELLINGTON
CAPE TOWN SALISBURY IBADAN NAIROBI DAR ES SALAAM LUSAKA ADDIS ABABA
BOMBAY CALCUTTA MADRAS KARACHI LAHORE DACCA
KUALA LUMPUR SINGAPORE HONG KONG TOKYO

---





PRINTED IN GREAT BRITAIN
BY BUTLER & TANNER LTD
FROME AND LONDON

# Acknowledgement

I am much indebted to my colleague in our Psychology department, A. W. MacRae. Without his help, I should not have known where to start in acquainting myself with recent work on the psychology and physiology of colour vision. He kindly set up apparatus to enable me to look at familiar objects lit by unfamiliar lights, and has been patient in answering questions and in correcting misunderstandings. But he is, of course, in no way responsible for any mistakes that remain, nor for the manner in which I have presented scientists' findings.

*University College of North Wales, Bangor*
June 1970

# Contents

# List of Figures

# Introduction

MOST contemporary English-speaking philosophers would endorse our common-sense convictions concerning perception. In this respect they are not a representative sample of the species *philosopher*. Most philosophers have embraced conclusions which violate the canons of common sense, and some of those who have professed to defend the views of 'the vulgar' have ascribed to the latter far-fetched theories. The main concern of this book is to consider whether our common-sense convictions can be justified. If they cannot, the alternative theories between which we seem obliged to choose are all paradoxical, and are very hard to believe when one is using one's sense-organs and not just thinking about their use. These theories will not be examined in detail, for presumably few would wish to embrace any of them without first doing his utmost to defend our common-sense beliefs. When I speak thus of 'common-sense beliefs (convictions, etc.)', I use such expressions, as philosophers commonly do, to refer to beliefs which are generally accepted in their own culture as needing no justification, as being so obviously true that one rarely finds occasion even to formulate them.

It is sometimes said that a philosopher's function is to cure a certain kind of perplexity. Questions concerning the philosopher's function and the nature of his concern with perception will be discussed in Part Three. Here we may simply note that only those who have suffered perplexity need to be cured of it. Puzzlement about perception only begins when we have recognized reasons for doubting or rejecting our common-sense convictions. An introduction to the philosophy of perception must induce some perplexity. This is the function of Part One which sets out at some length the arguments against common-sense Realism. Students of the history of philosophy may be astonished to find how short and thin are the arguments which many philosophers have offered as sufficient to dispose of our common-sense assumptions. David Hume, for example, started by saying ' 'tis vain to ask, whether there be body or not? That is a point which we must take for granted in all our reasoning.'[1] Yet he rapidly reached the conclusion that this conviction cannot be justified since 'there is a direct and total opposition betwixt our reason and our senses', a conflict for which his only remedy is 'carelessness and inattention'. Hume's crucial argument for rejecting belief in 'the continued and independent existence of body' consists simply in mentioning these familiar facts: the kind of double vision which we experience 'when we press one eye with a finger', 'the seeming increase and diminution of objects according to their distance' and 'the apparent alterations in their figure', and the 'changes in their colour or other qualities from our sickness and distempers'. In order to decide whether such facts do have such drastic implications, the implicit reasoning must be examined with some care.

In Part One, I shall adopt the role of prosecuting counsel, in Part Two that of counsel for the defence, with common-sense Realism in the dock. In Part Three, I shall assume the role of judge. I shall not, however, follow the conventions of a debating society, in which one is free to use any argument or rhetorical device which may win a vote. In Parts One and Two, I have tried to obey the following rules: (i) to try to do equal justice to both sides of the case; (ii) not to waste a reader's time by using arguments which I regard as feeble or as mere sophistry; (iii) in presenting arguments used by others, to try to put them persuasively, but not at the price of suppressing what seem to me obvious weaknesses; (iv) in presenting each side of the case, to retain the same role throughout. In Part Two, I try to answer all the arguments presented in Part One. But since Part Two will contain some arguments which, I think, should not be accepted as decisive, I shall explain why I think this in the first two chapters of Part Three.

The structure of this book has some disadvantages, notably that it is a devious method for developing one's own theses. I hope, how-

[1] References, numbered consecutively for each chapter, are listed on pp. 181–6.

ever, that it has some advantages as an introduction to philosophy, both in exhibiting philosophy as a dialectical activity and in offering readers opportunities to exercise their own critical faculties. I urge readers to assess for themselves the successive arguments presented in Parts One and Two, and not simply wait to see how they are dealt with in the sequel.

I shall take account, to an extent not common in recent British philosophy, of empirical facts other than facts about English grammar. Evaluation of theories which have been designed to make sense of non-linguistic facts calls for critical attention to the relevant facts. Since perception is studied by several of the sciences, the philosophy of perception ought not to ignore their discoveries, and I shall discuss some important experiments on the psychology and physiology of perception.

Part One

# A Critique of Common-sense Realism

# 1

# An Introduction to Phenomenology and to 'the Sense-datum Language'

HOWEVER *observant* people are, in the normal sense of this term, there is a sense in which all of us most of the time and some of us all the time are very unobservant. When using our sense-organs, our attention is normally focused upon external objects, their properties and interrelations. Naturally, since our survival depends upon recognizing and adjusting our behaviour to the things in our environment. To illustrate the sense in which we are very unobservant, I shall give three examples. Do daylight and standard electric light bulbs always cast on white paper shadows which are of some shade of grey? Until recently, I should, without hesitation, have answered Yes. I had failed to notice something which must have stared me in the face on hundreds of occasions when in a certain situation: when writing at my desk with daylight fading I light a lamp, and two shadows of my pen are cast on the paper. The shadow then cast by daylight and lit by lamplight is of a buttercup yellow, and the other shadow is sky-blue, even when lit by a grey cloudy sky. Readers who have not noticed this phenomenon can easily verify it. The effect is most striking when the curtains are adjusted to admit only a chink of daylight, and the thing casting the shadows is so placed that both shadows are about equally dark.

Here is a second example. Presumably everyone has sometimes gazed for 15 seconds or more at a brightly coloured object. I do not suppose that anyone has thereby got the impression that the object was fading in colour before his eyes. Yet the *colour* one sees does change as one's gaze remains fixed. A simple experiment shows how much it changes. Gaze at the dot in the middle of the red rectangle on the cover of this book. After 15 or 20 seconds you should have noticed some dilution of the colour. To recognize how much the colour has faded, repeat the process with one eye closed. Then close this eye and open the other. The vividness of the red that you now see will be striking, and *very* different from the washed out shade that you had just been seeing with the other eye.

A third example to illustrate the sense in which we are so unobservant concerns double vision. A distinguished philosopher, J. L. Austin, has referred to double vision as 'a quite *exceptional case*' and 'a rather baffling abnormality'.[1] But for people with two eyes, double vision is an almost invariable feature of vision—in this sense, that one has double images of all objects visibly nearer, and visibly more distant, than that on which one's eyes are focused. To pay attention to objects on which one's eyes are not focused needs some, but only a little, effort. To do this is abnormal only in the sense that it is not done often or spontaneously. Failure to notice this feature of our visual experience mars many important contributions to the theory of vision. I shall give two examples.

In his *Essay Towards a New Theory of Vision* (1709), Berkeley started by posing the problem how we perceive by sight the distances (and shapes) of objects. This struck him as a problem because, he says, it is 'agreed by all, that *distance* of itself, and immediately, cannot be seen. For *distance* being a line directed end-wise to the eye, it projects only one point in the fund [retina] of the eye. Which point remains invariably the same, whether the distance be longer or shorter'(§II). As this quotation and his ensuing arguments reveal, Berkeley was assuming that what is visibly presented to us are two-dimensional patterns of colours. On this premise, the distances which we attribute to visible objects must be due to the mind interpreting its two-dimensional data, making inferences which have become so automatic that we are never conscious of making them. Berkeley insists that such inferences must be based on data of which we are, or can become, conscious. And according to Berkeley, the most important data are, not features of what we *see*, but the muscular sensations which we can, but rarely do, notice when we change the focus of our eyes. Berkeley was criticizing a strange theory, said by him to be 'the received opinion', that one recognizes the distance of an object by seeing the angle subtended *at the object* by a line from each eye. Yet, though he is criticizing a theory, and keeps appealing to his readers to test theories by attending to their own perceptual experiences, he never notices the double images which are nearly always noticeable when we are using our eyes. Nor did he notice another feature of our visual experience which enables us to see or judge the distances of things, namely parallax, the fact that when you move your head to the right, the images of nearer objects move to the left relative to the images of further objects. Berkeley's own odd starting point, that what we see are two-dimensional patterns of colours was a by-product of *his* theory. It was not the result of observation, in the everyday sense of "observation"* or any other sense.

The importance of double vision for depth perception was demonstrated in 1883 by Charles Wheatstone who invented the stereoscope. Yet here is a recent example of a contribution to the theory of vision being marred through ignoring double vision. It comes from an important series of experiments[2] conducted by the psychologist R. H. Thouless. One of these experiments concerned the 'apparent sizes' of objects located at different distances.[3] The subjects were asked to report when two discs 'appeared' or 'looked' the same in size. The larger disc remained 2·4 metres from the subject's nose. The smaller disc (its diameter three-quarters of that of the other) was moved closer to the subject, who was asked to say when the two discs were equal in 'apparent size'. The two discs were kept in visibly different directions from the subject. One of the four subjects did not give the expected response, even when the smaller disc was 'too near the subject for convenient measurement'. That this subject was right to refrain will be obvious to anyone who repeats the experiment. This can be done with two coins of different sizes. Place the larger upright about two yards away. Move the other to and fro by hand, and ask yourself Thouless's question, using both eyes as his subjects did. I think you will want to say that the coins *refuse* to look the

* I have in this book followed a convention which I have adopted in another book *A Critique of Linguistic Philosophy* (1970), where I explain why I think that some such convention is needed. I use double quotation marks to indicate that I am mentioning, and saying something about, a *linguistic expression as such* (a word, phrase or sentence). I use single quotation marks for the other purposes for which quotation marks are customarily used, notably to indicate that one is quoting a *statement* expressed in the very same sentence that its author had used to express it. When quoting, I do not alter the author's quotation marks when they do not conform to my rules.

same size, that "looking the same size" is just not applicable. Thouless's question becomes applicable, and easy to answer, if you close one eye. But with both eyes open you see the relative distances and sizes of the coins; for, whether you notice this or not, when you focus on the nearer coin you see twin images of the further coin, and *vice versa*. Once you have noticed the double images seen in such a situation, you may find it surprising that a psychologist investigating vision should overlook this phenomenon. Yet Thouless did, judging by the questions which he addressed to his subjects and his comments on their answers.

The reader may wonder whether what has been said so far is relevant to philosophy. It is, for our subject-matter is perception, and apart from their theoretical implications, which will be discussed later, the facts which I have mentioned illustrate several points. In any critical study of perception, it is important to pay close attention to the perceptual experiences which one is trying to describe and explain, to try not to let one's descriptions of the facts be distorted by a preconceived theory, or by one's beliefs about the physical properties of the things one perceives, or by failure to check the appropriateness of one's questions or answers by using one's own sense-organs. I recommend that readers should, whenever possible, check statements made in this and other books about how things look or appear under given conditions. Many frequently made statements can thus be found to be false, e.g. that if one wears green spectacles, a white object, or even everything, looks green. If one suspends one's normal perceptual preoccupation—with identifying physical things of familiar kinds, etc.—there is what we may call another 'dimension of perceptual experience'. If one starts paying heed to the contents of one's 'visual field', it is possible to go on noticing things that had never been noticed before.

How shall we designate this other dimension, and what language shall we use to report what we discover therein? These are matters for decision. The first decision is easy, for there is a word available, "phenomenology". I shall use this word, and shall speak of 'phenomenological attention and description'. Sometimes, to save ink, I shall use "phenomenal" instead of "phenomenological", and shall not use "phenomenal" in other senses. I shall be using "phenomenology" and "phenomenon" in the senses which the *Oxford English Dictionary* sought to define thus:

*Phenomenology* 'That division of any science which describes and classifies its phenomena';
*Phenomenon* 'In philosophical use: That of which the senses or the mind directly takes note; an immediate object of perception'.

As I use it, "phenomenology" will not carry commitment to any controversial theories, as it does for some continental philosophers, who would probably consider the kind of phenomenology that I shall practise too cautious.

The second decision poses problems which are much less simple. The OED definition of "phenomenon" suggests two alternative terminologies for giving phenomen(ologic)al descriptions, by using the expressions "*directly* take note of" and "*immediate* objects of perception". This reflects ways of talking which have been common among philosophers—qualifying "to perceive" and the verbs which name species of perception, "see", "hear", etc., by adding adverbs such as "immediately", "directly", "strictly", or sometimes "actually". Some philosophers have recently chided others for using such expressions. Austin has professed not to understand what A. J. Ayer meant by speaking of 'directly seeing' something. Austin reminded us that, in everyday talk, the point of saying that something is 'directly seen' would be to exclude cases like seeing it via a mirror or a periscope.[4] Ayer was not, of course, using the expression in this way, but as a technical term. Some technical terms are indispensable for the purpose of giving phenomenal descriptions. Everyday English provides no words which do this job unambiguously. This is not surprising, since natural languages have evolved to serve practical purposes. It is, however, desirable that what one uses as technical terms should not also be everyday expressions, like "seen directly", which invite, or provide scope for misunderstanding.

In giving phenomenal descriptions one may, and for the present I must, use certain terms which are not in everyday use: "sense-given" (given in sense-experience) and "sense-datum" (that which is so given). This choice is dictated by the fact that I must later expound and discuss theories of perception which, during the twentieth century, have been expressed in the terminology of 'sense-data'. In introducing any technical terminology, one needs to make decisions about the rules which are to be followed, and the rules should be adapted to serve the purpose(s) for which the terminology is introduced. My purpose in introducing a sense-datum language is to give phenomenal descriptions and prevent these from being confused with statements about the nature of the publicly observable things which are being perceived. It follows that "sense-datum" should be used to refer to what one is aware of when one is seeing, hearing, etc., and is suspending one's knowledge or beliefs about the material thing(s) which one is seeing or hearing; and that one should describe as 'sense-given' the properties which one is aware of when in this frame of mind. It is then appropriate to introduce a verb corresponding to "sense-datum" and "sense-given", namely "to sense", and to contrast sensing and perceiving. I shall speak of sensing, but not of perceiving or seeing, etc., a sense-datum, and of perceiving or smelling or touching, but not sensing, e.g. a pig. The use of the technical terms may be illustrated thus. When one sees and touches a tomato, what one is said to sense are 'a visual sense-datum' and 'a tactual sense-datum'. When I notice a bottle beyond the finger on which my eyes are still focused, I shall say that I sense two sense-data, but not, of course, that I see two bottles. When fixing my gaze on a tomato makes the colour fade, I shall say that the sense-given colour (or the colour of my sense-datum) changes, but not, of course, that I see the tomato changing in colour. To say that I see two bottles or that I see the tomato change colour would imply that I believe things that I do not believe.

There is another technical term which it is convenient to have available: the verb "to be perceptually conscious of". During the twentieth century, English-speaking philosophers have debated *ad nauseam* the use of English perceptual verbs like "to see". All would agree that "to see" is commonly used in such a way that 'John sees a dagger" implies that a dagger is physically present before John's eyes. Some say (recognize!) that it is correct, good English, to speak of a person seeing a hallucinatory dagger or pink rat. But some philosophers have denied this last statement. To avoid quarrels about English usage, we may use "to be perceptually conscious of" according to the following rules. Its grammatical object must be a name or description of some material thing or event, e.g. "a dagger" or "a peal of thunder". But to say that a person is perceptually conscious of a dagger is not to imply that there is a dagger affecting his sense-organs, or even that he *believes* this, but only that, like Shakespeare's Macbeth, he is having a perceptual experience which he has some inclination to interpret as seeing a dagger (or, unlike Macbeth, as touching a dagger). It is useful to have such a verb in order to describe the perceptual judgements which we classify as illusions and hallucinations. Philosophers who use "sense-datum" adopt a rule which we can now express thus: that whenever a person is perceptually conscious of something, he is sensing at least one sense-datum and is interpreting the latter as belonging to the thing of which he is perceptually conscious. Such philosophers have, however, disagreed, as we shall see later, about the nature of the relationship referred to here by "belonging to".

We must now acknowledge a motive for adopting a sense-datum language distinct from the desire to give phenomenal descriptions, though not unrelated to the latter motive. The concern of philosophers with perception has arisen largely from the fact that our perceptual judgements are quite often mistaken. This fact led Descartes to ask how we can avoid such errors, and to propound the principle that philosophy ought to start with the question: what is it *impossible* for me to doubt?[5] The philosophers who introduced the term "sense-datum" (though not the notion in question) were G. E. Moore and Bertrand Russell. Both made it clear from the start that their main motive was that of Descartes—the quest for incorrigible statements, which could provide foundations for a reconstruction, or a justification, of human knowledge. Moore used "sense-datum" in lectures given in 1911.[6] The question which he set out to answer in the lecture entitled 'Sense-Data' was: 'How do we know of the existence of material objects, supposing that, as common sense supposes, we *do* know of their existence?' Russell used "sense-datum" in the first chapter of *The Problems of Philosophy* (1912), which starts: 'Is there any knowledge in the world so certain that no reasonable man could doubt it?' Let us consider the direction in which one is led by a quest for incorrigible statements.

Suppose I say, on a dark night, 'I heard a mallard drake over there.' It is obvious that my claim goes far beyond my evidence. All that I *heard* was a couple of faint quacking sounds. I took it for granted that these emanated from a bird with a bottle green head, yellow beak, curly tail feathers, etc. I know from experience that such sounds usually originate from such a bird, but also that some people can imitate them. If I wish to avoid all risk of error, I must confine myself to describing what was sense-given, for which the onomatopoeic word "quack" is a fairly good description. In cases of perception by hearing, it seems reasonable to follow Moore in equating what is sense-given with what is 'actually' or 'strictly' heard. Suppose now that someone reports that he saw an orange lying in the wood, but passed it by without further inspection. Again, the claim goes far beyond the speaker's evidence, for it is true only if the thing he saw (had) contained juice of a certain familiar flavour and odour, if it grew on an orange tree, etc. It could have been verified by *vision* that it had grown on a tree, but not that it had a certain flavour or odour. If the speaker were pressed to confine himself to what he *saw* (actually or strictly)—as he might in a law-court if something hung on it—presumably he should say, e.g. 'I saw something round and orange-coloured'; though even that is too much if, by "round", he means spherical, i.e. the three-dimensional shape to which oranges approximate. What was sense-given was, at most, part of the surface of a spherical object. And even if the sense-given object was visibly bulgy, the physical object could have been part of an empty orange-skin, or a fungus.

Notice, however, that if our only purpose in making guarded statements is the Cartesian quest for the incorrigible, there is another way in which this goal may be achieved. Instead of saying 'I saw something orange-coloured, round in outline and bulgy', one might say 'I saw what I thought was an orange, what appeared to be an orange.' Is *this* sort of statement to be classified as a phenomenal description? Some recent philosophers have, in effect, answered this question in the affirmative. But this involves confusing two different activities: (i) describing what is *sense-given*; (ii) describing what one is *perceptually conscious of*, that is, the nature of the physical thing(s) which one thinks one is seeing or hearing, etc. That these are very different is obvious if one considers that statements which describe what one is perceptually conscious of may give us no information about what is sense-given. The statement 'I think I see my dog' may be based on sensing what we may, for brevity, call waggling-white-tail-like sense-data, or on sensing two patches of light (when I look into a dark room and his eyes reflect light coming from behind me), etc. Conversely statements about what is sense-given, e.g. 'I sense two round luminous sense-data about five degrees apart in a black background', may give no information about what the speaker is perceptually conscious of—if anything, for the speaker may not yet have any idea what sort of physical thing(s) he is seeing, or whether it is a hallucination or an after-image.

To use "phenomenal descriptions" to cover reports about what one is perceptually conscious of *and* about what is sense-given would be to telescope questions whose difference is important—very important if one is interested in perception, and not simply in grinding a particular philosophical axe, i.e. the thesis that everything we know or believe must be derived from incorrigible statements. Those who wish only to grind that axe can of course ignore questions about what is sense-given. For statements about what is sense-given could never be more certain than statements like 'I think I see a dog', or 'I hear what seems to me to be a duck'. No one can fail to know what he is *perceptually conscious of*—what, if anything, he thinks he is perceiving. Can a person fail to know what he is now sensing, what are the properties of his present sense-data? Philosophers have commonly made it part of their definition of "sensing" and "sense-datum" that one cannot fail to know this. This is an arbitrary decision. It is one which nobody would have made simply as a result of reflecting about his own perceptual experience, or by practising phenomenology. I shall apply "phenomenal description" only to statements intended to describe what is sense-given and not to those which describe the objects of perceptual consciousness. We need to distinguish statements about what is sense-given from perceptual judgements, for most of the arguments which are used to show that our common-sense convictions are untenable start from premises concerning what is sense-given. We need a sense-datum language, or some equivalent, in order to state the arguments which will be examined in the next chapter. But whatever terminology we use for this purpose, it should be *theory-neutral*. And what is meant by calling such a terminology 'theory-neutral' is that it enables us to discuss the rival theories of perception without begging the question, or prejudicing us, in favour of any particular theory. This need is acknowledged by some at least of the philosophers who use "sense-datum". We should not, therefore, adopt any rules for using "sense-datum" which rule out the truth of our common-sense assumptions, e.g. that what we are calling 'a visual sense-datum' *is*, very often, the front surface of a physical object.

I have said that we need a sense-datum language 'or some

equivalent'. But many contemporary philosophers would claim that everything that can be said in a sense-datum language can be said more simply and clearly with the help of everyday English verbs like "looks", "sounds", "feels", etc., or "appears", or "seems", that, for example, we may say, 'the tomato looks a paler red than it did 20 seconds ago' instead of 'the sense-given colour has changed'; and may say 'I seem to see two bottles' instead of 'I sense two bottle-like sense-data'. This is true, but philosophers who say this have commonly failed to notice that if "looks", "appears", etc. are to be used for expressing phenomenal descriptions, this use will be a technical one which requires explanation, and that rules for this technical use need to be specified. Indeed some of the same decisions which arise when one is introducing "sense-datum" will have to be made concerning this technical use of "looks", "appears", etc. Some of the philosophers who make it their business to describe English usage have recently acknowledged the variety of the uses we make of such verbs, have referred to 'the phenomenological sense' of such verbs, and have proceeded as if that phrase needed no explanation. Not unnaturally they sometimes confuse the use of such verbs to report what is sense-given with some of their other uses.

One use, and a very common use, of "looks", "appears", and "seems", is to give *estimates* about the objective properties of the physical things one is looking at. This, surely, is how we should, in most everyday contexts, interpret questions like 'Does this object look to you (or appear or seem to you to be) bigger (whiter or more distant) than that one?' A person who volunteers about some physical object a remark like 'It looks (or appears or seems to me to be) so and so' usually intends to convey thereby that his statement is *merely* an estimate, that he is not committing himself to its accuracy. (If he starts with "It looks", this implies that his estimate is based on what he now sees; if he starts with "It seems", this is not implied.) If we are using "looks" in the sense just described, a penny almost always looks round and smaller than a melon looks. In the phenomen(ologic)al sense of "looks", a penny usually looks elliptical and not infrequently looks larger than a melon looks. Are my last two statements sufficient to explain what is meant by "the phenomenological sense of "looks" "? Unfortunately not. If we left it at that, this use would remain very indeterminate. This point can be conveniently conveyed by considering the results of some of Thouless's experiments referred to earlier. But first I wish to adopt a convention which I shall follow throughout the remainder of this book. When I am using "looks" and kindred words in a phenomenological sense—in the sense in which pennies usually look elliptical—I shall indicate this by writing "$\text{looks}_{(\text{ph})}$" or "$\text{appears}_{(\text{ph})}$" or "$\text{apparent}_{(\text{ph})}$".

In order to convey to his subjects the questions which he wanted them to answer, Thouless used "looks", "appears", and "apparent". In one series of experiments, the subjects looked at a round disc lying flat on a table two or three yards away. They were asked to convey how its shape 'looked' or 'appeared' to them. In some cases the subjects had to draw the shape in question, in most cases to select the one which matched from a set of slightly different elliptical discs, when the latter were viewed from a line perpendicular to their surfaces. Thouless was well aware that verbs like "looks" are ambiguous. He told his subjects that he was not asking 'what the shape of the object really is nor how [the subject] thinks it ought to look but simply the shape it does look to him'.[7] There was, however, an astonishingly wide variation in the responses. To save words, I reproduce, with the kind permission of Dr. Thouless, the diagram which he used to illustrate this (Figure 1).

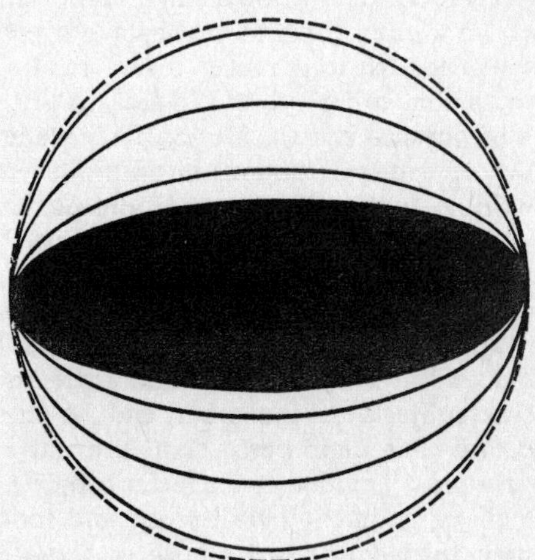

*Figure 1.* The range of variation in his subjects' responses to Thouless's questions concerning 'apparent shape'.

The dotted line shows the real shape of the disc. The black ellipse represents what Thouless called 'the perspectival shape', meaning the shape the disc projected on a vertical plane at or near the subjects' eyes, the shape which a camera would record if its lens lay in that plane. Of the three continuous lines, the middle one represents the average for the 'apparent shapes' reported by all the subjects, and the other two represent the limits of variation. Thus some subjects equated the 'apparent shape' with an almost circular ellipse, some with an ellipse whose vertical height was about half that of the latter ellipse.

On this evidence we seem to be obliged to conclude, as Thouless did, that when different people view the same thing in exactly the same conditions, how it $\text{looks}_{(\text{ph})}$ to them varies very widely. And not just in shape, for Thouless found a similarly wide variation in the responses when his subjects were asked to report on the 'apparent size' and the 'apparent brightness' of objects. Confronted with such facts, one is obliged to adopt *some* rule for using "$\text{looks}_{(\text{ph})}$". This could be that when a person reports how a thing $\text{looks}_{(\text{ph})}$ to him, whatever he says goes. And this is the rule which Thouless adopted in practice, without acknowledging that there are alternatives. One question which needs to be raised here is whether Thouless succeeded in conveying to all of his subjects the question which he wanted them to answer. He tried, but perhaps some of them still tended to confuse "looks" in the phenomenological sense with that other use of "looks", to give estimates of the properties of physical things. Alternatively we might suppose that subjects who grasped Thouless's meaning nevertheless failed to notice how things $\textit{look}_{(\textit{ph})}$ in the conditions of the experiment. Indeed there is some evidence in Thouless's report that the variations in his results were due to one or both of these factors. Thouless wrote, without discussing the implications, that subjects who classified the 'apparent shape' of a tilted disc as being nearly circular tended to 'show no surprise and little interest in the results', whereas subjects at the other end of the range were 'astonished to find that their perceptions are not exactly determined by the stimulus'.[8] Evidently the latter subjects did interpret "apparent" in the phenomenological sense, and took for granted something which turned out to be false *in those experimental conditions*. And notice that the conditions in most of Thouless's experiments made it as difficult as possible to suspend one's beliefs about the physical properties of the perceived objects. When you know that such a disc is round and you look at it with both eyes from a range of less than three yards, it is virtually impossible to discount one's knowledge of its physical shape, size, and distance. Yet even under these conditions, there are simple techniques which help one to recognize the sense-given shape of a thing, and we were taught some of them by our drawing masters, e.g. closing one eye and screwing up the other. Another technique is to compare the sense-given lengths of the horizontal and vertical axes of an elliptical shape, a comparison aided by holding a pencil at arm's length. A further technique is to look at the thing through a tube or a hole in a screen.

We are free then to adopt a rule for using "looks$_{(ph)}$", "apparent$_{(ph)}$", etc. according to which a person can fail to notice how a thing looks$_{(ph)}$ or appears$_{(ph)}$ even when he is trying to do this. In that case we should need a rule for deciding how a thing really looks$_{(ph)}$ to a person. We could adopt the rule that the shape that a thing really looks$_{(ph)}$ is what Thouless called its 'perspectival shape', and that the size a thing really looks$_{(ph)}$ is its 'field of view' size, meaning the proportion of one's visual field that it fills. Admittedly adoption of this last rule would be a somewhat arbitrary decision. But then so will any decisions which we make in introducing such technical terms. And there is something to be said for adopting a rule which enables us to give definite answers to how-does-it-look$_{(ph)}$ questions, instead of leaving such questions vague and adopting in practice the rule that whatever a person says goes. If we did adopt the alternative rules which I have suggested, we should want to stress that the ability to recognize how things (really) look$_{(ph)}$ requires some practice and skill, and that in some conditions this is very difficult, unless one uses special techniques. That phenomenal attention and description requires training and practice was a commonplace for earlier generations of psychologists who regarded introspection as their primary source of data. What we are calling 'phenomenal description' is a species of what they called 'introspective reports'.

Notice that the phenomenological use of verbs like "looks" is indispensable. It cannot be conjured away by 'analysis'. Suppose one tries. 'The penny looks$_{(ph)}$ elliptical' may be paraphrased as 'It looks like an elliptical surface seen from in front.' But this paraphrase uses "looks" in the phenomenological sense. It is a way of saying 'It looks $_{(ph)}$ as an elliptical surface looks$_{(ph)}$, when seen from in front.' Whatever rules one adopts for "looks$_{(ph)}$" (or for a sense-datum language), it is vital not to confuse "looks$_{(ph)}$" with the use of "looks" to give estimates of the objective properties of perceived objects. Thouless did this in some of his experiments.[9] These were experiments in which the subjects were asked to report when two pieces of grey paper, at different distances from a lamp, were equal in 'apparent whiteness'. Thouless had started off on the wrong foot by citing someone else's finding that the 'apparent hues' of things 'tend to remain constant in spite of changes in the illumination'.[10] This refers to the fact that people *estimate* pretty accurately certain properties of physical surfaces—their colours as seen in normal daylight; and that, despite the wide differences in the colours that a thing looks$_{(ph)}$ in different lighting, it may continue to look the same colour in the other sense of "look". Thouless began by asking his subjects to report on the apparent *whiteness* of the pieces of paper. Some of his subjects asked him whether he wanted to know 'when they look equally *bright* or when they look equally *white*'. So, in the second half of this experiment, Thouless asked both questions; but still failed to recognize the important difference between 'do they look equally white?' and 'do they look equally bright?' The former question would, I think, normally be interpreted as a request for an estimate of the 'real' colour or lightness of the things perceived, and "look" would not then be used in the phenomenological sense. The latter question would, presumably, be normally interpreted, when referring to objects and not lights, as a phenomenological question. That Thouless's subjects were confused by his questions is evident from their answers. Most of them gave widely different answers to the questions concerning whiteness and concerning brightness, but some gave very similar answers. Thouless's confusion is shown by the fact that he decided that the answers concerning 'apparent whiteness' were the ones comparable with his results for 'apparent shape' and 'apparent size'. But then he was not comparing like with like. He was comparing estimates of objective colour with phenomenal descriptions of shapes and sizes.

What psychologists have written about perception has often been clouded by failure to distinguish the different functions of verbs like "looks" and "appears". What they refer to by "size-constancy" is usually the familiar fact that e.g. a man looks (is recognized as *being*) man-sized, whether he is seen from two yards or from 200, despite the wide differences in the sizes he looks$_{(ph)}$. What is constant is the perceived, the estimated, size. As Descartes wrote in *Dioptrics*:

their [objects'] size is judged according to our knowledge or opinion of their distance . . . It is not the absolute size of the images* that counts. Clearly they are a hundred times bigger [in area], when the objects are very close to us than when they are ten times further away; but they [the images] do not make us see the objects as a hundred times bigger; on the contrary, they [the objects] seem [i.e. seem to be, not seem$_{(ph)}$] almost the same size, . . . so long as we are not deceived by distance.

Yet R. L. Gregory, having just quoted this passage from Descartes, describes Thouless as measuring 'the amount of constancy under various conditions'.[11] He presents Thouless's experiments as if the subjects had been asked to *estimate* the real sizes and shapes of objects! † Thouless may also have done some such experiments; others have. But the experiments to which Gregory here refers us are those which I have described. What Thouless's results show is

* Descartes was here referring to the sizes of the so-called retinal images, but what he says would be applicable if he had been giving a phenomenological description and referring to field-of-view sizes.

† Gregory's only hint that this is not what Thouless asked his subjects to do is his statement: 'From the actual sizes [of the objects which the subjects were looking at], the amount of size constancy could easily be calculated' (*Eye and Brain*, p. 153). But this statement suggests a serious error—that of assuming, without evidence, that a person's competence in estimating the real sizes (or shapes) of things can be deduced from his incompetence in recognizing their field-of-view sizes (or perspectival shapes). Thouless is partly responsible for this error being made. His caption for Figure 1 above was 'Tendency to constancy of shape'. It is, however, only by experiments designed for the purpose that we could discover whether, for any particular person, the two different abilities are negatively or positively correlated. Some people possess both abilities to a high degree, e.g. those who are skilled *both* in driving cars or aeroplanes *and* in arts like photography or perspectival drawing. Psychologists have commonly failed to distinguish two very different senses which have been given to terms like "size-constancy": (*a*) the more or less constant *perceived* sizes of familiar types of physical object, and (*b*) the tendency of reports of *phenomenological* size to be influenced by (*a*). This obscures the fact that individuals vary much more in respect of (*b*) than they do in respect of (*a*). (This footnote is addressed primarily to psychologists. Thouless's experiments are often cited by psychologists, but I have not found any account of them which does not misdescribe them.)

that when people are asked how things $look_{(ph)}$, their answers are influenced to a very variable extent by what they estimate to be, or recognize as, their real properties. Psychologists' accounts of so-called object-constancy or phenomenal regression are ambiguous unless we are told, as often we are not, exactly what questions were addressed to their experimental subjects. (The philosophical relevance of this excursion into psychology will become clear later.)

I regret that my introduction to 'the sense-datum language' has had to be rather complicated. I cannot conscientiously introduce "sense-datum" as this has usually been done, e.g. simply by saying that a sense-datum is the sort of object whose existence and nature you cannot doubt when you look at a tomato or hear a noise; or by saying that whenever a thing *looks* so and so, there is a sense-datum which *is* so and so. The points which I wish most to stress are these: (i) that we need *some* technical terms for giving phenomenal descriptions and preventing these from being confused with statements of different types; (ii) that this can be achieved either by using terms like "sense-datum" or by using everyday words as technical terms, but that if we choose the latter policy we still have to decide on the rules for this technical use of words borrowed from everyday language; (iii) that whatever technical terminology we adopt, its rules ought to be theory-neutral. This last point requires, for example, that we should *not* follow G. E. Moore in using "sense-data" to include so-called mental images—pictures in the mind's eye and after-images. Such images are called 'mental' because we think that they cease to exist when their owner ceases to be aware of them. The view that the data of normal vision and touch are like mental images in this respect has been supported by arguments which we must examine, but it should not be infiltrated by using the same name for both. Incidentally some recent writers speak of 'the Sense-datum Theory of Perception'. This is misleading. All theories of perception can be, and most have been, expressed in a sense-datum language. In order to remind readers that talk about sense-data can usually be translated into statements about how things $look_{(ph)}$, $sound_{(ph)}$, etc., I shall in the sequel alternate between these two technical terminologies. In using "$looks_{(ph)}$", "$appears_{(ph)}$", etc., I shall follow the rule that when a person reports how something $looks_{(ph)}$, whatever he says goes. The elasticity which we have discovered in 'the phenomenological use of "looks"' should not be forgotten; but it need not be taken into account for our present purpose, namely to formulate the stock arguments against our common sense assumptions concerning perception.

# 2

# Phenomenological Arguments against Realism

IN his classic introductory book, *The Problems of Philosophy*, Bertrand Russell required only about 1,500 words to reach the conclusions that what we are 'immediately aware of are sense-data' and that 'the real table, if there is one, is not immediately known to us, but must be an inference . . .' I shall proceed more slowly. The first step will be to formulate the relevant features of those common-sense convictions which we should not think of questioning unless exposed to philosophy or science, and which are presupposed in our everyday uses of language. To simplify exposition, I shall use "physical object" to mean a three-dimensional solid which is tangible and relatively stable, e.g. a mountain, a mushroom, or a grain of sand. Physical objects, in this sense, form a large and important class of the things that we perceive, and this class includes one's own body. I shall not follow those philosophers who use "external objects" to refer to the objects of perception, since this suggests that their own bodies are being excluded. We perceive many things besides physical objects in the sense defined, e.g. thunder, the sky, fog, flames, shadows, running water, etc. I shall use "physical thing" to include the latter as well as physical objects. For our purposes, it is not necessary to decide just *how* stable a physical thing need to be to qualify as a physical object, for example, whether a raindrop or a spark from a fire so qualifies.

The following tenets of common sense must be mentioned, since reflection about perception has led some philosophers to deny the literal truth of each of them.

(1) *The existence of things in physical space:* that there are

physical objects, each of which has, at each moment of its existence, a determinate location in a single three-dimensional space.

(2) *The accessibility of physical objects to different sense-organs:* that the same physical object is accessible to sight and to touch, and also in many cases to hearing and/or smell and/or taste.

(3) *The immediacy of vision:* that when one is looking with the naked eye at a physical object, say a tomato, the round red object (the so-called sense-datum) *is* a surface of the tomato.

(4) *The immediacy of touch:* that when one is touching a physical object, e.g. holding in one's hand a tomato, the smooth cool expanse (the so-called sense-datum) *is* part *both* of the surface of the tomato *and* of the surface of one's hand.

(5) *The accessibility of physical objects to different observers:* that the *same* physical object can be perceived by any normal human observer who is suitably placed.

(6) *The continuous existence of physical objects:* that a physical object continues to exist during the intervals when it is not being perceived by anyone.

(7) *The resemblance between observed and unobserved physical objects:* that when a physical object is not being perceived, it still possesses the kinds of properties which we do or can perceive it to possess.

(8) *The possession of causal powers:* that physical objects possess causal powers whereby they interact with each other whether or not they are being perceived.

When formulating statements designed to apply to all modes of perception and all kinds of perceptible properties, one's generalizations are liable to be *too* general. This applies to my formulation of tenets (2) and (7). These need to be supplemented by pointing out that a physical object is accessible to different sense-organs in different senses of "accessible", that an object possesses different kinds of perceptible properties in different senses of "possesses". We assume that what we see and touch *are surfaces of* the tomato. Does anyone think that the smell it makes when grilled or the noise it makes when it hits the floor are possessed by the tomato in *this* sense? Presumably not. Any noises or smells which it 'possesses' are surely possessed by it only in the sense that it plays a part in causing them, in making us experience them.

Philosophers often speak of 'Realism' as a theory of perception, or, if they reject this theory, they call it 'Naïve Realism'. They often fail to make clear which of the tenets of common sense they intend 'Realism' to embrace. I shall use "Realism" to refer collectively to all of the eight tenets listed above; and I shall speak of Realism as a theory. This would be inappropriate if it implied that the plain man regards any of these tenets as problematical. Of course he doesn't. He takes them for granted and finds no occasion to formulate them. Still, a philosopher who is considering whether, and how, these tenets can be justified, is entitled to describe them as constituting one theory among others.

The arguments against Realism to be expounded in this and the next chapter are commonly referred to, indiscriminately, as 'the Argument from Illusion', as if they were all variations of a single theme. I shall not follow this habit. Its main source is in the manner in which Descartes presented his case for doubting the existence of all material things. In his first *Meditation*, Descartes produced an argument of breath-taking brevity. This may be paraphrased as follows:

(i) All of my beliefs concerning material things are based on the testimony of my senses;
(ii) I know that my senses have sometimes deceived me;
(iii) Therefore my senses may always deceive me;
(iv) Therefore there may be no material things;
(v) Therefore I may have no senses.

All the facts which Descartes cited in support of this argument were presented as cases of a person being 'deceived by his senses'.

As it stands, the pattern of Descartes' argument exposes it to obvious criticisms. Consider the premise which I have numbered (ii). Though Descartes did not acknowledge this point, this premise must start with 'I know that', for he is applying his policy of doubting everything which is not known with absolute certainty. We should therefore ask *how* he can know that his senses have sometimes deceived him. Suppose he referred us to one of his own examples, that of a tower 'which at a distance seemed round, [but] appeared square when viewed more closely'. If Descartes was claiming to *know* that he was deceived by his eyes when 'at a distance', he must have been assuming that his eyes did not deceive him when at closer quarters. More generally, to *know* that my senses have deceived me on any particular occasion, I must be relying on the testimony of my senses on some other occasion(s). If my evidence that a tower which I had taken to be round is really square consists of your spoken testimony, I should be relying on my ears not deceiving me in hearing what you said, and on your eyes not deceiving you when you looked at the tower. Can we then dismiss Descartes' argument? Not yet, for he could have amended it and said: I know that at least one of my beliefs about the tower must be false, for they are incompatible, and to know this I need not know whether the tower is really round or square or perhaps some other shape. And this, perhaps, is how he was thinking, for he does not say that he *saw* the tower's shape at closer quarters, only that it then 'appeared square'. Descartes still seems guilty of a gross inconsistency. Arguing from the premise 'My senses sometimes deceive me', he reaches, at the end of the first *Meditation*, the conclusion 'I may have no senses'! He could, however, have avoided this inconsistency by expressing himself more carefully: replacing "senses" by "sense-organs" in the conclusion and by "sense experiences" (or "sense-data") in the premise. This is how he was thinking. He is here entertaining a hypothesis, which he later claims to disprove, that it is causally possible for him to have sense-experiences without having sense-organs or indeed having a body. Descartes was preoccupied with the fact that we are fallible, and that our senses sometimes deceive us; but the arguments based on his own examples need not hinge on the fact that our perceptual judgements *are* sometimes mistaken, but rather on what provides the opportunity, and the temptation, to make such mistakes—the fact that a thing observed under different conditions appears$_{(ph)}$ to have *incompatible* properties.

I shall now present one of the stock arguments against Realism. If you look at the face of a penny from different viewpoints, the corresponding sense-data vary widely in all of their properties: in shape, from being round to being the thinnest of ellipses; in size, from being a just noticeable dot to filling the field of vision of one eye; in colour, from being black when the penny is held against the light to being shiny-white when it reflects a bright light, and although, occasionally, the sense-datum is almost uniformly brown, more often it presents a pattern of different shades of brown. A description of such familiar facts forms one premise of the argument, but two more are needed, and they seem so obvious that they are often not formulated. They are: (*a*) that a rigid object like a penny, unlike e.g. a cat, has a single real shape, and a single real size and that each part of its surface has a single real colour; (*b*) that we cannot, merely by looking at such a thing, make it change *its* shape (as we might in the case of a cat) or *its* size or *its* colour(s). The argument based on these premises (and are not all of them *facts*?) is as follows. Since the penny retains a single specific shape, size and colouring, and since the corresponding sense-data vary so widely in their shapes, sizes and colours, it is impossible to identify most of the sense-data with the surface of the penny. The same surface of the same physical object cannot simultaneously be round *and* elliptical, black *and* brown *and* shiny-white. Now when the penny looks$_{(ph)}$ to you black and elliptical, *something really is black and elliptical*—the object in the middle of your visual field. We cannot conjure away such objects by calling them 'mere appearances'. We need a noun like "sense-datum" to refer to such an object. Since the penny itself is round and of (a) certain shade(s) of brown, all of the sense-data which are not round or not brown must be entities of a different nature from the surface of the penny with which we had, uncritically, been identifying them.

A variation of this argument used by H. H. Price is based on variability of apparent$_{(ph)}$ size and shape, ignoring colour. It may be called 'the argument from perspectival distortion'. The conclusion which Price drew is that, when, for example, we look at a match box from different viewpoints, the different sense-data do not 'fit together' to form the surfaces of 'one single three-dimensional whole'.[1] His thought may be expressed by saying that if one cut pieces of cardboard to match each of the sense-data sensed when looking at each side of the box, these would not fit together to form a single box like the one we had been looking at. This draws attention, however, to a way of answering his argument. We could throw away most of the pieces of cardboard, and still select sets of these which fit together, namely those which match the sense-data obtained when viewing each surface of the match box from a line perpendicular to that surface and from the same distance for each surface. Thus Price's argument, as he recognized, does not show that *no* visual sense-datum can *be* the surface of a physical object, but only that *most* cannot.

Further arguments are needed to show that it is illegitimate to identify with a physical surface even those sense-data whose qualities coincide with the 'real' qualities of that surface, e.g. the round brown sense-datum sensed when the penny is viewed from in front, and in diffused lighting. Let us follow Price and Ayer in calling such sense-data 'veridical'. The second stage of the argument which I am presenting takes two forms: (i) that there is no intrinsic difference in kind between sense-data which are and those which are not veridical—for example, that there is no intrinsic difference between an elliptical black sense-datum obtained by looking at a brown penny held slanted against the light and one which is obtained by looking at a black elliptical disc held untilted against the light; (ii) that sense-data which are not veridical form *continuous* series which join up with sense-data which are veridical—for example, if you keep your eye on a penny as you move it about, there is, in Price's phrase, a 'sensibly continuous transition' between a sense-datum which is round and brown and one which is black and elliptical. Each successive shade is marginally darker, each successive shape marginally less circular. The black elliptical sense-datum cannot be the surface of the penny. And if we suppose that the round brown sense-datum *is* the surface of that external object, we should expect some detectable change at the point in the series where we stop seeing the penny and start seeing something else. Since we can detect no such change, it is unreasonable to treat a few privileged sense-data as *being* the surface of the penny, and we must conclude that all sense-data are entities of a different nature.

In expounding the above arguments, Price and Ayer have used the term "illusory sense-datum" as the opposite of "veridical sense-datum" without explaining clearly their use of either term.[2] What they meant by "illusory sense-datum" was presumably something like this: a sense-datum which has a specific shape (or colour, etc.) such that *if* one took this to be the real shape (or colour) of the perceived object one would be mistaken. It seems better, however, to dispense with the word "illusory" in this context. "The Argument from Illusion" is a very misleading title for the arguments to which it is applied. Consider those which I have just expounded. When looking at pennies, people scarcely ever suffer illusions, e.g. believe that the coins are elliptical. Even if they did, this would do little to strengthen the case against Realism—it would merely reinforce the second stage of the argument by supporting the thesis that there is no qualititative difference between sense-data which are and those which are not veridical. "The

Argument from Phenomen(ologic)al Variability" is a much more appropriate title for many of the arguments traditionally lumped together as 'the Argument from Illusion'. The arguments in question are based on the fact that the sense-data which are ascribed to the same physical object vary and possess *incompatible* properties.

The factors upon which phenomenal variability depends may be distinguished, and the relevant arguments classified according to the types of factors to which we attribute the variation, namely:

(1) External conditions, including:
  (*a*) the observer's viewpoint, i.e. the relative positions of his sense-organs and the object perceived;
  (*b*) the relative position and nature of the light-source(s) and the nature of the light(s);
  (*c*) the nature of the medium, or the presence of other things, between the observer and the object perceived.

(2) Internal conditions:
  (*a*) the states of the observer's sense-organs, nerves and brain;
  (*b*) psychological factors such as the observer's fears, hopes or expectations.

The arguments against Realism already expounded involve phenomenal variability due to factors of types (1)(*a*) and (*b*). Let us now consider some arguments where it is factors of type (1)(*c*) which are involved. First, the hard-worked case of the straight stick which looks$_{(ph)}$ and sometimes looks bent when partly immersed in water. This example should not, I think, be shrugged off by saying: we all know that sticks look bent under these conditions and know the explanation in terms of the bending of light waves, so we are not deceived. It is only too easy to deceive people by arranging sticks, some bent where they meet the water, at varying angles to the water, and asking them to judge by sight which sticks are really bent, and in which direction, and by how much. However, even if people were capable of making such estimates with any accuracy, this would not affect the argument. Its crux is that when one looks at the half-immersed stick (if it is not vertical) *something really is bent*, and sometimes very bent, by up to about thirty degrees, namely an object in the middle of one's visual field. So we need a noun like "sense-datum" to refer to this object; which cannot *be* the stick's front surface if the latter, as we can verify by touch, is straight.

Another case where variability is due to a factor of type (1)(*c*) is that of reflections. The argument is usually presented thus. An object 'seen in a mirror' (as we say) is visibly located at a certain distance behind the surface of the mirror. There is no such object in the place in question, so what is visibly located in this direction is a sense-datum which is not a surface of a physical object. Another way of putting the argument is this. Suppose that one is simultaneously seeing a ball, uniformly coloured and illuminated and viewed against a black background, and seeing one or more reflections of this ball. The mirrors may be invisible and the reflections indistinguishable from the ball as seen directly.* We need some noun which can be used in the plural to indicate the two or three somethings which are being seen. We are using "sense-datum" for this purpose. The perceptual experience in the present case may be described by saying that one is sensing several indistinguishable visual sense-data which are located in different directions. Then it would be self-contradictory to identify each of these sense-data with a surface of the same ball since, by definition, a physical object cannot be in different places at the same moment. To cap this argument, we need, of course, to add that if one of the sense-data were, and the others were not, a surface of the ball, we should expect to find some intrinsic difference between them.

Also attributable to factors of type (1)(*c*) is the phenomenal variability involved in using optical instruments, like telescopes, microscopes and spectacles, which can make immense differences to our sense-data, to the way things look$_{(ph)}$ (and look). Seen through a microscope, a thing which had looked red may look grey, and a surface which had looked smooth and shiny may look like a mountainous landscape. Now we are disposed to believe that magnification reveals what the surface of a thing is really like. And with good reason, for a glass which magnifies × 2 enables us to see the texture of a surface a little more clearly—and so on each time you double the magnification. But if a microscope reveals the real shape of a thing's surface, how can we also attribute to the

* The mirror-image of a familiar asymmetrical object may, of course, be recognized as such by virtue of the left–right reversal.

latter the very different shape it looks when we use the naked eye? If the surface of the table is really shaped like a range of mountains, it cannot also be really smooth. And then we must note that microscopes of different power reveal shapes which look very different. What degree of magnification reveals the real shape or texture of a surface? Any answer would be arbitrary. We seem obliged to conclude that different optical instruments make us sense different and very dissimilar sense-data when we are, as we say, looking through them 'at the same thing'.

There is another way in which the medium may cause phenomenal variability. The presence of pure clear air, when there is enough of it, greatly alters the colours things $\text{look}_{(\text{ph})}$. A distant mountainside $\text{looks}_{(\text{ph})}$ blue or purple. Indeed, does it not sometimes *look* (appear *to be*) blue or purple? At any rate, it may be impossible to recognize or infer, solely from what one now sees, whether the surface one is looking at is covered with green grass, purple heather or grey rock. Now let us turn to cases where phenomenal variability depends on the state of the observer's body. Double vision is a case in point. The kind of double vision referred to in the last chapter is normally ignored by philosophers. The kind which they discuss is when *everything* is seen in duplicate as a result of squinting or pressing one eyeball. J. L. Austin, who acknowledged no difficulty in disposing of other arguments against Realism, described such double vision as baffling. Both kinds of double vision provide an argument against Realism, but is the argument based on double vision different in principle from one which I based on mirror images? With the help of mirrors two indistinguishable sense-data may be sensed in different directions. This is what we experience in double vision.

A Realist may be tempted to dismiss double vision by saying that there is no problem, that we see one bottle double(d) or see it as two, or alternatively, that we see one bottle 'but looking double'. The former answer (Austin's)[3] will not do. Being double(d) or duplicated cannot be a property of what *still is* a single bottle, any more than being a pair of twins can be a property of a single person. We may of course say, with R. J. Hirst,[4] that a bottle 'looks double', but then we must acknowledge that we are using "looks" in a sense different from that in which we say either that it $\text{looks}_{(\text{ph})}$ multicoloured in this lighting, or that it looks half-full. For "looks" is then being used in an existential sense: "looks double" deputizes for "there appear to exist two bottles in different directions". We need a noun which can be used in the plural to refer to the two somethings, e.g. "image" or "sense-datum". Perhaps the reason why Austin found double vision, but not reflections, baffling was this. In the case of reflections we know or can easily find out which of two similar sense-data is in the direction of the bottle; whereas, in double vision resulting from squinting, there are no possible grounds for selecting *one* of the twin sense-data as the surface of the bottle or as being in the right direction. The crux of the present argument against Realism is that a physical object cannot be simultaneously located in two distinctly different directions from a particular place; that in double vision there are no grounds for identifying either of the twin sense-data with the perceived object, and that we are therefore obliged to conclude that neither sense-datum is a surface of the bottle.

Another popular example of the dependence of phenomenal variability on the state of the sense-organs is one used by John Locke: that if one hand has been immersed in hot, and the other in cold, water, and both are then plunged into tepid water, the latter feels cold to one hand and warm to the other. More difficult, I think, for a Realist to dispose of are cases where phenomenal colours change as a result of the conditions of the observer's eye or brain. It is reported that, to a person who is suffering from severe jaundice or who has taken certain drugs, everything looks$_{(ph)}$ yellow (though I suspect that it is only light-coloured surfaces of which he would say this). And there is the fact mentioned in the last chapter that while you fixate on a brightly coloured surface, the sense-given colour fades. If you gaze at the black spot in the centre of one of the coloured rectangles on the cover of this book, you will see the fading colour fringed by a margin of the original shade. The fading is due to chemical changes in the colour-receptors in the retina, to be discussed later, the fringe to one's inability to prevent slight eye-movements. A more surprising discovery has recently been made by a psychologist, Ivo Kohler. He wore spectacles with each lens half red and half green, so that when he turned his eyes to the *left* everything looked$_{(ph)}$ red and when to the *right* everything looked$_{(ph)}$ green. After a time things began to look$_{(ph)}$ their normal colours. But when he removed the spectacles everything to the *right* looked$_{(ph)}$ red and everything to the *left* green. This effect must presumably be due to adaptation in the brain, not the retinas, for it is related to the position of the eyes in the head and not to differences in the stimulation of the different halves of each retina.[5] Such facts strongly suggest that the colours that we see are not inherent qualities of the surfaces of physical objects. I shall not develop this argument further at present, since we shall have to return to it later.

It is easy to illustrate phenomenal variability due to psychological factors. Price cites the person who sees the "5" on a bus as "8", because he is expecting a number 8 bus. More interesting are the ambiguous figures which abound in psychology textbooks, which you cannot help seeing *as* one or other of two incompatible three-dimensional shapes. For example, you see either a flight of stairs from below or a similar flight from above, either two black faces on a white background or a white vase on a black background. While you see it in one way you *cannot* see it the other way, and then suddenly it changes and you cannot then see it in the first way. Must we not conclude from such facts that the visual sense-data cannot be identified with the relevant physical objects, since the latter are two-dimensional patterns on a page, whereas the sense-data have a three-dimensional pattern?

The last argument against Realism to be presented in this chapter is based not upon phenomenal variability but upon hallucinations. But first we need to draw a distinction not drawn in everyday language. As the *OED* records, "hallucination" and "illusion" may be used interchangeably, and they often are. This obscures a distinction which, for our purposes, is important, namely between:

(*a*) cases where a person perceives what is an external thing but he makes a mistake about the kind of thing it is or about its location, and this is what I shall mean by "illusion"; and

(*b*) cases of 'the apparent perception of an external object when no such object is present', as the *OED* defines the relevant use of "hallucination".

To avoid ambiguity we want to make "illusion" and "hallucination" mutually exclusive terms. For this purpose, the *OED* definition of "hallucination" may be elaborated thus: 'perceptual consciousness of a certain kind of physical thing as being located in a place where there is no physical thing, or reflection or projection thereof, to be mistaken for a thing of that kind'.

The implications of these definitions may be illustrated by pointing out that one type of mirage should then be classified as an illusion, and another type as a hallucination. When a desert traveller sees trees visibly located on the horizon but is sensing sense-data which belong to trees *beyond* the horizon, as a result of the bending of light waves by layers of hot air, this will count as an illusion. If the desert traveller, crazed with thirst, sees an oasis in a direction in which there is nothing, above or beyond the horizon, except flat sand, this will count as a hallucination. There is a third type of mirage which illustrates a difficulty in making "illusion" and "hallucination" mutually exclusive in their application. When one seems to see a pool of water at the end of a long road, one might classify this as a hallucination on the ground that there is no physical stuff on the road, or reflected by it, to be mistaken for water, *or* might classify it as an illusion on the ground that the sky (or light-waves) reflected by the road are being mistaken for water. I think, however, that my definitions of "illusion" and "hallucination" are sharp enough for our present purpose; if not for all possible purposes.

A further matter for decision is whether we should use "hallucination" only in cases where a person accepts false beliefs about what he is perceiving. This is the standard use. But for our purpose, the key question is not whether a person is deceived. One may never have been fooled by the pool-on-the-road type of mirage, yet the sense-data are like, perhaps very like, those sensed when one is seeing a pool on a road. I shall extend "hallucination" to include cases where a person is not deceived, but where his sense-data incline him to accept a false belief about what he is perceiving, because they are similar to normal sense-data; that is, to sense-data obtained when perceiving a physical thing of the relevant kind. 'Similar to normal sense-data', but how much similarity is required? This is crucial. The core of the present argument against Realism is this: *that there are cases where hallucinatory sense-data are indistinguishable from normal sense-data,* that both must therefore be entities of the same nature, that since hallucinatory sense-data are, by definition, not surfaces of physical objects and must be entities of a different nature from the latter, the same goes for normal sense-data.

Notice that the first, indispensable, premise of this argument is a *factual* claim. It would be frivolous to present as a reason for rejecting Realism the mere fact that the occurrence of hallucinations is *possible*. Yet Ayer* has argued thus—presumably because he had adopted the doctrine that 'philosophical analysis' has no concern with empirical facts.[6] Since the argument from hallucination does depend upon a factual premise, some care must be taken in establishing its truth. We ought to be cautious about drawing paradoxical conclusions from evidence which consists of the testimony of other people. Those who have experienced hallucinations, in the sense defined above, are not dependent upon such testimony. But I am, and shall assume that this is true of most readers. To support the factual premise of the present argument, we should not expect philosophers to rely upon works of fiction or the testimony of people who are mentally unbalanced. Yet the cases which they most frequently cite concern Macbeth's dagger and pink rats seen by a person suffering from *delirium tremens*. That the latter sometimes does not distinguish pink-rat-like sense-data from normal sense-data is evident from his behaviour. But when a person is ridden by fear, 'he does not distinguish . . .' scarcely guarantees 'they are indistinguishable'.

We need not dismiss the testimony of people under the influence of so-called hallucinogenic drugs, if there is good evidence that their critical faculties are unimpaired. It seems misguided, however, to present the effects of taking mescalin as providing a strong case against Realism, as J. R. Smythies does.[7] For, on Smythies' account, it is when the subjects' eyes are closed that they report visions of quasi-material objects; and when their eyes are open, the effect of the drug is to intensify the colours of the things seen and to endow some of them with great beauty and significance. There is, however, a good deal of relevant testimony from people who, on the evidence, are level-headed and were, at the time, in a normal state of mind. The annals of the Society for Psychical Research record many such cases. Judging by the 400-page *Report of the Census of Hallucinations*,[8] hallucinations are not all that rare: almost 10 per cent of a sample of 1,700 people claimed to have had a hallucination involving sight or touch or hearing. I shall give a short account of a hallucination which involved both sight and hearing.[9] We are not here concerned with the fact that it

* *The Problem of Knowledge*, London and New York, 1956, p. 98. Ayer also presents 'the argument from illusion' as requiring, *not* 'that the appearance of a physical object should ever actually vary', but only 'that it is possible that it should' (p. 95).

seemed to involve telepathy, which is what led to the case being investigated and well-documented.

On 7 December 1918, at 3.25 p.m., Lieut. David M'Connel crashed and was killed while piloting a plane from Scampton. In a letter written two weeks later, his friend Lieut. Larkin described his experiences on the afternoon of the 7th at the Scampton air-base. Having described M'Connel's departure, he wrote:

> I was certainly awake at the time, reading and smoking. I was sitting . . . in front of the fire, the door of the room being about eight feet away at my back. I heard someone walking up the passage; the door opened with the usual noise and clatter which David always made; I heard his 'Hello, boy!' and I turned half round in my chair and saw him standing in the doorway, half in and half out of the room. [Then after describing his dress and appearance] I remarked 'Hello, back already?' He replied, 'Yes. Got there all right, had a good trip.' I am not positively sure of the exact words he used . . . I did not have a watch, so could not be sure of the time, but was certain it was between a quarter and half-past three because shortly afterwards Lieut. Garner-Smith came into the room and it was a quarter to four. He said 'I hope Mac (David) gets back early . . .' I replied 'He *is* back, he was in the room a few minutes ago.'

When Larkin was told that evening about M'Connel's death, he assumed that it had occurred on a flight made after he had, as he thought, seen him. Next day a fellow officer tried and failed to convince Larkin that he could not have seen M'Connel the previous afternoon. There is written testimony from two officers confirming that the contents of Larkin's letter matched what he had told them before any of them had heard of the crash. In such a case, there are good reasons for thinking that hallucinatory sense-data were indistinguishable from normal sense-data. We do not have to rely on what the percipient said later, since his behaviour at the time displayed his convictions. So far as its logical form is concerned, the argument from hallucination does not depend upon people actually being deceived. Still, the most convincing evidence that someone's hallucinatory sense-data were indistinguishable from normal sense-data is his conviction that it was a case of normal perception.

Hypnotically induced hallucinations are sometimes cited in arguing against Realism. Caution is needed since psychologists use "hallucination" very liberally, even applying it to cases of *not* perceiving what is there, 'negative hallucination'. This phenomenon is common enough without help from hypnotists, and it does nothing to establish the premise of the argument which we are considering. Moreover, many of the cases which psychologists call 'positive hallucination' turn out to be illusions, in our sense, e.g. when an army private is made to see his Colonel as a Jap soldier and to try to strangle him. Some experimenters, however, have tried to answer a question crucial for our purpose: whether, in hypnotically induced hallucinations, the subject is *seeing* things which are not there, and not merely behaving as if he did. Consider an experiment by M. T. Orne, in which he compared the responses of hypnotized subjects and of 'faking subjects', i.e. subjects who had been told to simulate the behaviour of hypnotized subjects and try to fool the experimenter.[10] In one such experiment, a second experimenter, E, sat in full view of the subject, S, until S's eyes were closed. Then E moved silently to a position behind S. The hypnotist (Orne) told S that when he opened his eyes he would see E still sitting in the chair. After the hypnotized S had given every indication that he saw E in the empty chair, he was told to turn round and was asked 'who is that behind you?' Orne reports that almost invariably the genuinely hypnotized subjects looked back and forth several times and then said 'that they were perceiving two images of the same person'; and that when questioned about this, 'they tended to give bland responses such as "mirrors" or a "trick" '. The faking subjects never reacted thus. Either they declined to report seeing E behind them, or, having seen E there, they claimed that the hallucinatory E had vanished from the chair. Thus the reactions of Orne's hypnotized subjects strongly suggest that hallucinatory and normal sense-data were for them indistinguishable.

A classical example of hallucination, cited by Descartes, is what may be called 'the phantom limb phenomenon'. People who have had a limb amputated commonly continue after the operation, sometimes for many years, to feel pains in the missing limb, and sometimes also to feel tactual sensations therein. On regaining consciousness after the operation, patients are often deceived, and try to move or touch the aching leg and are astonished to find it has gone. But even when they know it has gone, they are for a time prone to forget this and to try e.g. to scratch an itch in a place occupied by air or blankets. Such behaviour combined with their testimony is formidable evidence that their hallucinatory sense-data are indistinguishable from normal sense-data. The common-sense assumption is that a pain is literally located in a (perhaps vaguely bounded) region of one's body, and that a tactual sensation is literally located in a specific part of one's skin. Can these assumptions be defended in view of the phantom limb hallucination? Here, a person is perceptually conscious of, and feels pains and tactual sensations in, a limb which is not there. We are not entitled to dismiss this case by invoking what doctors call 'referred pains', that is, where a pain is 'mislocated' in the sense that the place where it is felt is not that of the damaged or inflamed tissue which is causing the pain. We must distinguish the location of a sensation from that of its cause. The person who has a sensation is surely the authority about *its* location. It would be silly to say 'perhaps the pain (itch, pressure, etc.) which you feel in your heel is really in your thigh'.

The phantom limb hallucination presents a formidable challenge to common sense. Does it not show that perceptual judgements of kinds which we want to classify as incorrigible knowledge may be false; that bodily, including tactual, sensations are not physically located where we feel them, that the tactual sensations which one feels in a finger are not really in this physical object? Moreover, the phantom limb phenomenon indicates an answer to a question which I have hitherto suppressed. The conclusions of the arguments presented in this chapter have been that visual and tactual sense-data are not surfaces of physical objects, and must be 'entities of a different nature'. Then what *are* they? The phantom limb sense-data are caused by irritation of nerve-endings at the stump. They could presumably be triggered by stimulation of the appropriate nerves at any point on their way to the brain. Then presumably sense-data are produced by brain-processes. This brings us to the topic of the next chapter.

# 3
# Science-inspired Arguments against Realism

THE arguments presented in the last chapter are based on reflection concerning perceptual experience as such. They might have occurred, and some of them did, to people who believed that the function of the brain is to cool the blood. The arguments to be considered next are based on what scientists have learnt about the causes of perception, the functioning of our sense-organs and brains, and the nature of matter. I shall start, however, by considering a short passage written by John Locke late in the seventeenth century which much influenced the thought of later philosophers: chapter 8 of Book 2 of his *Essay Concerning Human Understanding*. Locke describes this passage as a 'little excursion into natural philosophy', i.e. into science. I shall formulate in the sense-datum language three theses which Locke has usually, and I think correctly, been interpreted as advancing here:

(i) that the qualities of sense-data can be divided into two classes, 'primary' and 'secondary', primary qualities including shape, size, position, and motion, secondary qualities including colour, sound, odour, flavour, and warmth and coldness as felt. (Notice that the so-called primary qualities belong only to some species of sense-data, notably visual and tactual);

(ii) that in respect of the primary qualities of any sense-datum, the physical object thereby perceived has similar qualities—'their patterns do really exist in the bodies themselves';

(iii) that in respect of the secondary qualities of any sense-datum, the physical object thereby perceived does not possess these qualities, but only the power to produce in us sense-data which possess them; and that such powers depend only on the primary qualities of bodies, on 'the bulk, figure, texture and motion of their insensible parts'.

In the interests of readers who have read, or will read, Locke, I shall now draw attention to the language in which Locke expressed these theses. (Other readers could skip this paragraph.) In Locke's language, theses (ii) and (iii) are expressed by saying that 'ideas of primary qualities' resemble 'the primary qualities of bodies', and that 'ideas of secondary qualities' do not resemble 'the secondary qualities of bodies'. Locke used "idea" for many other purposes, but when discussing perception he normally used it as we are using "sense-datum", to refer to what he called 'the immediate object of perception'. Locke inadvisedly defined "quality" in such a way that only bodies and not 'ideas' (sense-data) have qualities. He wrote: 'the power to produce any idea in our mind I call *quality* of the subject wherein that power is'. So when he speaks of 'the primary (or secondary) qualities of a body', this should mean the body's power to produce in us sense-data which possess the features in question. However, because Locke held that a body has a shape, size, etc., like those of the 'ideas' it produces, he normally used "primary qualities of bodies" to refer, not to powers in the bodies, but to the inherent shapes, sizes, etc., of bodies. And because he held that no *body* is coloured, warm, sweet, etc., he used "secondary qualities of bodies" to refer to their powers to produce in us 'ideas' which have colours, thermal qualities, etc. Locke did not, however, succeed in conforming to his own ill-chosen technical terminology. For this failure he apologized in advance (§8). He acknowledged that he sometimes speaks as if 'ideas' were 'in the things themselves'. He did not, however, notice that he sometimes slips into using "qualities" to mean, not powers to produce ideas, but warmth, colours, sweetness, etc., which are what other people would call 'sensible qualities', qualities which, on his own account, belong only to sense-data. (See § 14 and 16). In subsequent philosophy, the terms "primary" and "secondary qualities" have usually been used, not as Locke defined them, but I have used them in formulating Locke's three theses. (The orthodox interpretation of Locke's theses which I have presented has recently been challenged by A. D. Woozley,[1] who suggests that, in interpreting what Locke says about perception, we should read "idea of" as meaning 'thought of'. But if one tries to apply this proposal in detail, the difficulties are, I think, obvious and acute.)

Locke was well aware that his theses fly in the face of common sense, yet the arguments which he offers in their support are few and flimsy. One reason why I am starting this chapter by discussing Locke's excursion into science is to make it clear that his theses cannot be disposed of, as some philosophers have supposed, simply by rebutting Locke's arguments; a task incisively performed by Berkeley. Locke offered no arguments for thesis (ii). Indeed, quite often he uses Realist language when speaking of primary qualities, e.g. 'such as sense constantly finds in every particle of matter which has bulk enough to be perceived'. He says also that the primary qualities of a body are 'utterly inseparable from it'; and later that they constitute the essence of a body, which, on his own account of "essence", means that "body" is defined in terms of primary qualities. Locke's arguments for thesis (iii) are as follows:

(*a*) We think that the pain felt by a person who is too close to a fire is in him, not in the fire, so we ought to think the same about its warmth.

(*b*) 'Hinder light but from striking on it [a piece of porphyry, marble], and its colours vanish . . . Can anyone think any real alterations are made in the *porphyry* by the presence or absence of light; and that those *ideas* of whiteness and redness are really in the *porphyry* in the light, when it is plain *it has no colour in the dark*?' (Locke's italics).

(*c*) 'the same water, at the same time, may produce the *idea* of cold by one hand and of heat by the other, whereas it is impossible that the same water, if those *ideas* were really in it, should at the same time be both hot and cold'.

Locke followed Galileo in using the last of these arguments to support the hypothesis that 'warmth as it is in our hands' is '*nothing but* a certain sort and degree of motion in the minute particles of our nerves' (my italics). But if heat in one's hand is identified with molecular motion therein, inorganic bodies and fires can, in the same sense, be hot. We should have expected Locke to argue here that warmth as felt is wholly different in kind from the motion of hypothetical particles, such motion being, on his own account, a primary quality. Berkeley interpreted Locke's arguments as an appeal to phenomenal variability, and he offered a simple answer to the use of any such argument to show that primary qualities are, and secondary qualities are not, real (inherent) properties of bodies; namely that such arguments apply with equal force to primary and to secondary qualities.[2] Berkeley's point may be applied thus. If anyone claimed, as Locke had not, that the sense-data ascribed to a body vary in their secondary qualities, e.g. colour, but not in their primary qualities, e.g. shape, this is manifestly false. Applying Berkeley's point to Locke's argument concerning the colours of the porphyry, the obvious retort is: 'Hinder the light from striking it and its shape, size, etc., vanish as well as its colour.'

Later in his *Essay* (2.2.23), Locke used another quasi-scientific argument to support thesis (iii). He says that the 'now secondary qualities of bodies would disappear if we could discover the primary qualities of their minute parts'. His argument is that blood, seen through a microscope, appears as 'only some few globules of red, swimming in a pellucid liquor', and he surmises that we should no longer see anything red if we used a more powerful instrument. The obvious answer to this is that "colour" should here include the so-called neutral colours, white, grays and black, as Locke elsewhere recognizes. Then nothing could appear at all, when one looks through a microscope, unless one saw different colours in different directions.

It seems scarcely credible that Locke should have thought that his arguments were sufficient to establish his thesis concerning secondary qualities. The explanation is, I think, that Locke saw himself as simply purveying some scientific knowledge. What he says about primary and secondary qualities is his way of expressing conclusions which had been reached by Galileo, Boyle, and Newton. Galileo had expressed Locke's thesis (iii) thus:

> these tastes, odours, colours, etc., on the side of the object in which they seem to exist, are nothing else than mere names, but [I] hold their residence [to be] solely in the sensitive body [that of the percipient]; so that if the animal were removed, every such quality would be abolished and annihilated.[3]

Boyle rightly objected to Galileo's saying that, considered as attributes of external objects, secondary qualities are 'mere names', and he said instead that they exist in a body as 'a disposition of its constituent corpuscles', such that, if a sensitive organism is affected thereby, the disposition 'would produce . . . a sensible quality'.[4] What Boyle called 'a disposition', Locke called 'a power', but unfortunately *also* called it 'a quality' and even 'a sensible quality'.

We must try to understand why many scientists and philosophers have felt obliged to endorse the three theses which Locke presented so unclearly. The first stage is to recognize why scientific accounts of perception indicate that our sense-data exist only in us. The reasoning in question is reflected in what Locke treats as wholly uncontroversial. He frequently speaks of 'ideas' and 'sensations' being *produced in us*, and he tells us how they are produced, i.e. by 'modes of motion in our animal spirits variously agitated by external objects'. (He assumed that nerves are sheaths containing rarified stuff called 'animal spirits'.) Locke asserts that bodies must produce ideas in us 'by impulse, the only way we can conceive bodies [to] operate in'. Locke took it for granted that any perceptual experience is preceded by a continuous chain of causes—corpuscles emanating from an external object, striking a sense-organ, thus causing pressures in animal spirits which travel to the brain. The scientists' account of the transmission processes has changed, but this is not here relevant. They still agree that perception depends upon physical processes which terminate in a brain. We seem to be obliged then to conclude, like Locke, that the terminal processes produce sense-data *in us*. As Russell has said, any perception comes at the end of a chain of physical events leading from the object to the brain of the percipient; so we cannot suppose that at the end of the process, the last effect suddenly jumps back to its starting point, like a stretched rope when it snaps. The common-sense assumption is that a tactual sense-datum is always, and a visual sense-datum often, a surface of a physical object. But how can it be, since it is 'the last effect', something 'produced in us'?

R. J. Hirst has argued that, if we consider the transmission processes and the fact that they take time, we must conclude that 'the final events . . . occur in the thing or substance last affected [i.e. the brain] . . . that they come into being in the percipient . . . and do not exist in the object which is the remote beginning of the causal chain'.[5] But later in his book, Hirst tries to avoid this conclusion. 'We must', he says, 'either say that seeing or hearing the object is *the whole causal process* or that it is the end-stage of it' (p. 133, my italics). And Hirst chooses the former alternative. This commits him, however, to some embarrassing conclusions. For example, that my seeing the sun takes about eight minutes, the time taken for light to travel from sun to earth. Worse still, Hirst would have to say that my seeing a distant star takes a much longer time than I have lived. Russell's statement, that we cannot suppose that the last effect jumps back to its starting point, has special force here. It is known that stars sometimes explode and disintegrate. It is a statistical certainty that some of the stars that we see have disintegrated during the millions of years since the light now reaching our eyes left them. Suppose this is true of the star at which you are now looking. Is it not obvious that you cannot identify the twinkling point of light which you now see (or the round non-twinkling object that you could perhaps see through a powerful telescope) with the star itself? *Ex hypothesi*, there *is* now no star in the place in question. The star which (as we say) you now see, is merely the remote cause of what you see; that is, of what you are sensing, for surely we are obliged to describe the twinkling object in your visual field as a sense-datum which is produced in you. Or will you be so bold as to reject one of the most firmly established laws of physics —that light travels at about 186,000 miles per second? Otherwise you are obliged to abandon some of your common-sense assumptions, e.g. that the setting sun is where you see it, just above the horizon, and not already below it.

Of the philosophers who conclude that sense-data are produced in us, some, including Locke, have concluded that sense-data exist 'in the mind', some, like Russell and Hirst, that they exist 'in the brain'. Whether a philosopher will find either of these phrases apt, and if so which he will prefer, will depend on his views concerning the mind-body problem, which cannot be discussed here. The point to be stressed now is that there is a great deal of evidence that the immediate cause of a person's sensing any sense-datum is some physical process in his brain. Is such a process merely a necessary condition, or is it a *sufficient* condition, of the sensing of a sense-datum? If it is a sufficient condition, sense-data should be experienced if appropriate processes occur in a person's brain without any relevant stimulation of his sense-organs. If scientists could, by artificially stimulating a person's brain, make him experience visual and tactual sense-data, this would surely be decisive evidence that such sense-data are not what common sense assumes them to be, but are fleeting by-products of cerebral processes. And this has apparently been done.

The facts in question are sometimes referred to as 'artificially induced hallucinations'. I have heard a distinguished philosopher say in a lecture that, by stimulation of one's brain, one can be made to see an absent friend or a table that is not there. Such statements are premature, to say the least. The relevant facts are reported by brain surgeons, who have interrogated patients whose cortex was exposed, and who had been given only a local anaesthetic. This is usually a preliminary operation, to help the surgeon decide how much tissue to sever when removing a tumour. An electrode delivering 40 or 80 pulses per second is applied to different parts of the cortex. Such stimulation of regions involved in the control of muscles often causes involuntary movements of the patient's limbs, while stimulation of the 'sensory areas' of the cortex usually makes the patient experience sensations. Wilder Penfield, a pioneer of such experiments, has described his findings in two important books.[6] He tells us how his patients described the sensations thus induced:

> he reports a sensation of tingling or numbness, or of movement of a particular part [of his body]. But he is never under the impression that he has touched an external object . . .
> the subject variously describes the sound as ringing, humming, clicking, rushing, chirping . . . He is never under the impression that he has heard words, nor music, nor anything that represents a memory.
> . . . what the patients see is much more elementary than things seen in ordinary life. They have described what they saw as "flickering lights", "colours", "stars", "wheels" . . . "coloured balls whirling" . . . (p. 36).

It does not seem appropriate to describe such experiences as 'hallucinations' as I am using this term. On the other hand it seems more appropriate to describe them as sensing sense-data, rather than as having (mental) images. Or perhaps the conclusion should be that the distinction which a Realist wishes, and needs, to draw between sense-data and mental images, disintegrates in the light of Penfield's findings. When a certain region of the cortex (the temporal lobe) was stimulated, patients reported what some of them called 'a flash-back'—the involuntary reliving of some past experience, which unfolded at its natural pace so long as the electrode was held in place (pp. 45–55). Patients described such experiences as 'seeing again' and 'hearing again', and not as re-membering. All agreed that these quasi-perceptual experiences were much more vivid than those involved in normal memory. Some commented on a paradoxical sense of 'doubling of awareness', i.e. of being simultaneously aware of their location on the operating table while seeing and hearing absent friends.

If, by titivating their brains, people could be made to be perceptually conscious of whatever the experimenter wished, a Realist would surely have no leg left to stand on. Nothing like this has been done. Yet. However, the techniques used so far are crude —electric shocks disturbing many adjacent brain-cells. No doubt more delicate methods will be developed. Perhaps even enabling an experimenter to make me see and hear A. J. Ayer giving a lecture? In any case, the facts now available support the conclusion that sense-data are like mental images in that both are transitory by-products of cerebral processes. Notice that this conclusion renders intelligible facts mentioned in the last chapter which are otherwise hard to explain: the dependence of visible colours on the state of the percipient's body, and the phantom limb hallucination. Sensations felt in, or on the surface of, a limb no longer there are presumably created by brain-processes and 'projected', interpreted as belonging to other parts of one's body.

So far we have been concerned with the grounds for concluding that sense-data are 'produced in us'. We must now consider the case for ascribing to physical things primary but not secondary qualities. Contemporary philosophers commonly underestimate the strength of this case, which is often attributed to a tendency on the part of scientists to make a metaphysic out of their method, as E. A. Burtt has put it.[7] This seems to be a justifiable comment on the early fathers of physics, notably Kepler and Galileo, who were led by the success of their method of discovery, to conceive of the physical universe as a mathematical harmony and of God as the master mathematician. Their method, which was more explicitly formulated by Newton, was to single out from the phenomena to be explained certain key properties, measurable properties; to search for equations as simple and comprehensive as possible in which only these properties were represented, equations which fitted all the observed facts and which could be tested by deducing from them further phenomena whose occurrence could be verified by observation or controlled experiments. This method was magnificently successful in leading to the formulation of the laws of mechanics. For this purpose the only properties of things which had to be taken into account were mass, position, and speed, and one unobservable something, 'the force of gravity'. Kepler and

Galileo concluded that the only real (inherent) properties of matter are those which figured in their equations, and Newton also affirmed this view, though less dogmatically.

Galileo and Newton accepted the atomic theory of matter. The properties which Newton ascribed to the atoms included hardness and impenetrability. Then a critic may ask: since some sense-given qualities like degrees of hardness are ascribed to atoms, why not others like colours? The same question could have been addressed to the Greek atomists like Democritus, who, in the fifth century B.C., maintained that nothing exists except atoms and the void, and that the only objective properties of an atom are its shape and size, positions and speeds. As an atom was conceived by both Democritus and Newton, it is the sort of thing which *could* be coloured—a three-dimensional solid. If being too small to be visible permits it to have a shape of a *kind* which is visible, surely it permits its having a colour. Why did even Democritus who, so far as we know, did no measuring, conclude that secondary qualities are subjective and a by-product of the primary qualities of atoms? (Democritus imaginatively explained an acid taste in terms of angular, small, thin atoms.) What influenced Democritus, Galileo, and Newton seems to have been simply the thought that it is *superfluous* to ascribe to matter any properties other than primary qualities. They seem to have been applying a principle formulated by William of Occam (Occam's Razor)—that entities should not be multiplied beyond what is necessary, or rather a corollary of this—that we should attribute to entities no more properties than are necessary, necessary, that is, for the purpose of scientific explanation. That Newton was thinking on these lines is confirmed by his first rule for reasoning: 'We are to admit no more causes of natural things than such as are both true and sufficient to explain their appearances . . . for nature is pleased with simplicity and affects not the pomp of superfluous causes.'[8] Then the case for denying that secondary qualities are inherent in material things is very weak. The motions of things conform to laws which mention only some of their perceptible properties. This does not show that they do not *have* their other perceptible properties. 'Not measurable' does not imply 'not real'.

The case for Locke's thesis concerning secondary qualities was weak when he wrote his *Essay*. Since then it has become very strong indeed. In a nutshell, it is that there are innumerable empirical facts, otherwise unintelligible, which have been rendered intelligible by scientists, and that scientific theories explain such facts in terms of entities, fields, or forces *to which secondary qualities cannot intelligibly be ascribed.* To convey the strength of the case, there is, unfortunately, no short-cut which enables us to ignore the kinds of explanation offered by science. Let us concentrate on colour, the kind of secondary quality most important to most of us, both aesthetically and also for acquiring knowledge about the world. It is no accident that, in discussing perception, philosophers have been concerned primarily with vision, for vision yields more detailed and discriminating information than our other senses, and it is vision which provides the main puzzles.

The simple initial experiments which Newton describes in *Optiks* force us to look critically at the Realist's assumption that colours inhere *inter alia* in surfaces of physical objects (*inter alia* because the sky, for example, is not a physical object). Newton found that when a beam of light is passed through a prism we see, spread out, the colours of the visible spectrum; and that by recombining light from any two bands of the spectrum, one of the other spectral colours is made to appear. He worked out laws which enable us to predict the visible colour produced by mixing lights selected from any two or more different parts of the spectrum, and he designed a simple diagram which represents all of these laws, the colour circle (see Figure 2). This led Newton to conclude, initially, that 'it can be no longer disputed . . . whether they [colours] be qualities of the objects we see . . . since colours are the qualities of light, having its rays for their entire and immediate subject . . .'[9] But later he went further and concluded that colour-qualities cannot literally be ascribed even to light. In *Optiks* he wrote:

> If at any time I speak of Light and Rays as coloured . . . I would be understood to speak not philosophically and properly, but grossly, and according to such conceptions as vulgar people . . . would be apt to frame. For the Rays to speak properly are not coloured. In them there is nothing else than a certain Power and Disposition to stir up a Sensation of this or that Colour.[10]

When writing carefully, Newton commonly spoke of red-*making* or blue-*making* rays.

The reason why Newton took this further step and located colours *in us,* was that he supposed that the colours that we see

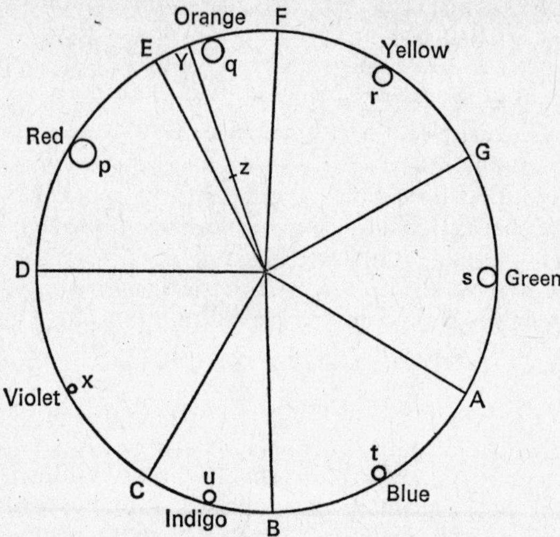


*Figure 2. Newton's colour circle.*

In *Optiks* (Prop. iv. Prob. 11), Newton explained his diagram thus:

> With the Centre O and Radius OD describe a Circle ADF, and distinguish its circumference into seven parts. . . . Let the first part DE represent a red Colour, the second EF orange, the third FG yellow, the fourth GA green, the fifth AB blue, the sixth BC indigo, and the seventh CD violet. And conceive that these are all the Colours of uncompounded Light gradually passing into one another, as they do when made by prisms; the circumference . . . representing the whole series of Colours from one end of the Sun's colour'd Image to the other, so that from D to E be all degrees of red, at E the mean Colour between red and orange, from E to F all degrees of orange, at F the mean between orange and yellow, from F to G all degrees of yellow, and so on. Let p be the centre of gravity of the arc DE, and q, r, s, t, u, x, the centres of gravity of the Arches EF, FG, GA, AB, BC, and CD, respectively, and about those centres of gravity let Circles proportional to the number of Rays of each Colour in the given Mixture be describ'd; that is, the Circle p proportional to the number of red-making Rays in the Mixture, the Circle q proportional to the number of the orange-making Rays in the Mixture, and so of the rest. Find the centre of gravity of all those Circles p, q, r, s, t, u, x. Let that centre be Z, and from the centre of the Circle ADF, through Z to the circumference, drawing the right Line OY, the place of the Point Y in the circumference shall show the Colour arising from the composition of all the Colours in the given Mixture, and the Line OZ shall be proportional to the fulness or intenseness of the Colour, that is, to its distance from whiteness. As if Y fall in the middle between F and G, the compounded Colour shall be the best yellow; if Y verge from the middle towards F or G, the compounded colour shall accordingly be a yellow verging towards orange or green.

are determined by the 'several bignesses' of the 'vibrations' of the light stimulating our eyes, 'the shortest Vibrations . . . making a Sensation of deep violet, . . . the largest . . . making a Sensation of deep red'.[11] Newton adopted this hypothesis tentatively, since he could not prove it, but it was an inspired guess. Newton was, however, supposing that what vibrates are light-*particles.* Then it would have been conceivable, though gratuitous, to suppose that the particles whose different vibrations make us see red (or violet) shades are themselves red (violet), though invisible. But the subsequent development of physics makes that supposition unintelligible. Light-waves are now known to be a very small slice of the spectrum of electro-magnetic radiation, whose wavelengths range from over a mile to less than $\frac{1}{40{,}000{,}000{,}000}$ of an inch. The slice to which our eyes respond comprises less than one octave, the wavelengths being in the order of $\frac{1}{50{,}000}$ of an inch. It is electro-magnetic radiation differing from light-waves only in the size of the respective wavelengths which transmits to us the heat of the sun, which is used to transmit music on the radio, which penetrates our bodies and enables radiologists to take X-ray photographs. Electro-magnetic radiation—fluctuations in electrical potential—is not the sort of thing that could have the colour-qualities which pervade regions of one's visual field. It would be absurd to suggest that such radiant energy, when of certain wavelengths is literally coloured, when of certain wavelengths literally warm, and so on.

Physics has made it unintelligible to ascribe the colour-qualities which we see to light-waves. A Realist may retort that he has never wished to ascribe colours to light-waves, but rather to things like tomatoes; that what he believes is that a tomato reflects 'red-making rays' *because it is red,* and that Newton need not have abandoned this position. Though this route was perhaps open in 1700, it is now blocked. The point to be stressed here is not that ascription of colour to tomatoes, etc., can play no part in scientific explanation, though that of course it true. It is that there is no single property corresponding to their visible colour in the various physical objects which look or look$_{(ph)}$ the same colour. To explain this point it is necessary to say something about the physiology of colour-vision. Our ability to see colours is due to the fact that our eyes contain photo-chemical substances, which respond differently to different wavelengths and are segregated in different receptors. The retinas of most humans contain large numbers of each of four types of receptors. There are the rods which are much more sensitive than the cones and which enable us to see in dim lighting and to see only the so-called neutral colours. There are three types of cones, each very selective in their responses: one type most sensitive to the longer (red- and yellow-making) wavelengths, one to the medium (green-making) and one to the shorter (blue- and violet-making) wavelengths. That this is so was tentatively suggested by Thomas Young in 1802, and until recently the hypothesis, though widely accepted, had not been directly confirmed. This has recently been done by experiments of great delicacy. At Cambridge, W. A. H. Rushton plotted the relative absorption of different wavelengths by the red- and the green-making pigments, by measuring lights which had been reflected through the foveas of colour-blind people.[12] At Johns Hopkins University,[13] Edward F. MacNichol and others passed light through individual cone-cells of men and monkeys, and measured the proportions of the different wavelengths absorbed therein. Figure 3 shows the results of the work at Johns Hopkins. Such measurements involve a large margin of error, but they agree fairly well with curves for the sensitivity of the colour receptor systems in humans which have been derived by complex calculations from the data of colour-matching tests.[14]

The experimenters have found, incidentally, that the cones which are most sensitive to long wavelengths respond more to wavelengths which make us see yellows than to the still longer wavelengths which make us see reds. However, most of the experimenters, including Rushton and MacNichol, have continued to speak as if the cones in question are (primarily) responsible for making us see reds. Rushton christened the light-sensitive pigment in such cones "erythrolabe", meaning 'red-catching'. Such language is, however, liable to mislead, apart from the fact that "catching" here suggests Naïve Realism. To speak of the red-, green- and blue-catching (or -making) pigments suggests that each cone-pigment reveals (or makes) a *single* spectral colour. This is gratuitous. What matters, presumably, is the *differential* absorption of each wavelength by the one, two or three types of cones affected thereby. As Figure 3 shows, lights which look blue-green affect each of the three types of cones, and lights which look orange affect two types.

Other things being equal,* two light-stimuli make a person

* The qualifications buried by this phrase will be exhumed later.

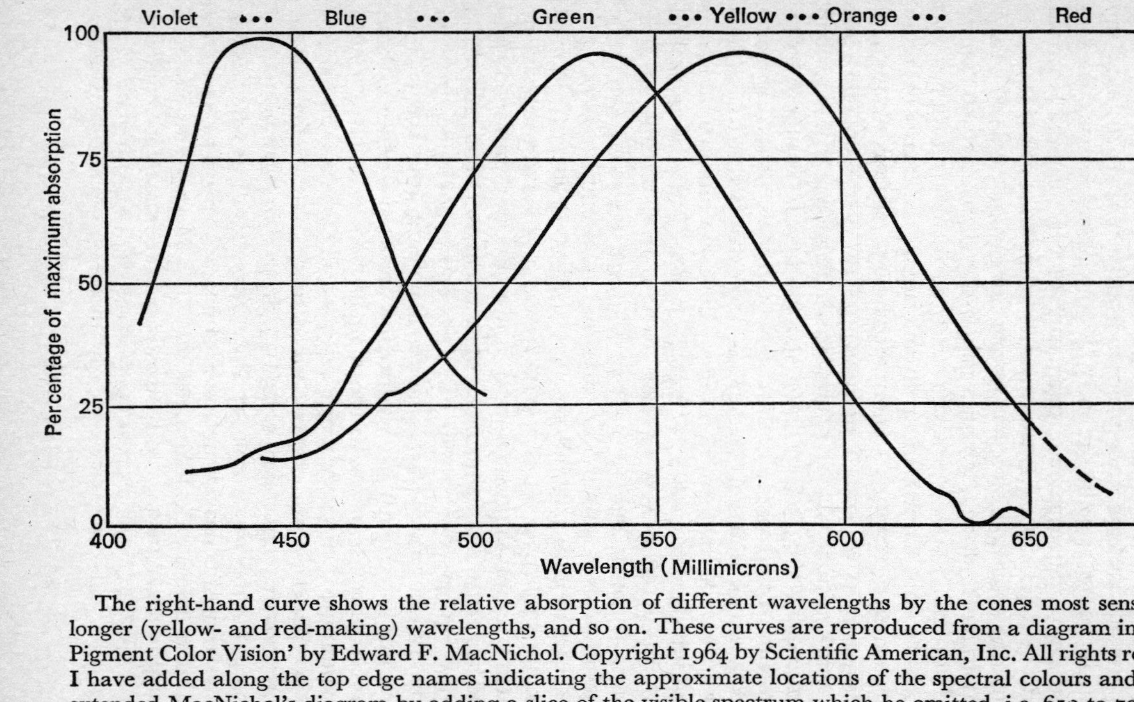


The right-hand curve shows the relative absorption of different wavelengths by the cones most sensitive to longer (yellow- and red-making) wavelengths, and so on. These curves are reproduced from a diagram in 'Three Pigment Color Vision' by Edward F. MacNichol.  I have added along the top edge names indicating the approximate locations of the spectral colours and I have extended MacNichol's diagram by adding a slice of the visible spectrum which he omitted, i.e. 650 to 700 millimicrons.

*Figure 3. Spectral absorption curves for the three cone-pigments in primates.*

sense two sense-data indistinguishable in colour, if each of them stimulates his three types of cones *in the same ratio*, e.g. 3 : 4 : 1. But this same end-result may be produced by an infinite number of different mixtures of different wavelengths. Consider a surface which, as we say, is white. Such a surface reflects unselectively all wavelengths in the incident light. It looks white if it is reflecting daylight or any artificial light which is like daylight in containing roughly equal proportions of all wavelengths. Such light is not needed, however, to make such a surface look white. Illumination by *any* mixture of wavelengths which stimulates the three types of cones in roughly the same proportions as daylight does will make the surface look white. There are innumerable mixtures which fill this bill, some containing only two specific wavelengths, which, separately, make us see e.g. yellow and blue. Now what has been said about things looking white goes for any other colour. There is an infinite number of different mixtures of wavelengths whereby you can be made to see each of the colours that you can see.

The proportions of the different wavelengths which a physical object reflects are determined by its molecular structure in and near its surface. Two objects may be very different in their molecular structure, and the light which each is reflecting may therefore contain different proportions of the different wavelengths in the incident light, yet the two different mixtures may be equivalent so far as our cones are concerned, that is, in stimulating the three types *in the same proportions*. Thus objects indistinguishable in colour under the same lighting conditions may be, and commonly are, very different in respect of their relevant physical properties. The proportions of different wavelengths which a surface is reflecting can be discovered by using a spectrometer. This instrument plots, wavelength by wavelength, the percentage of the incident light which a thing is reflecting; and thereby gives a physicist much information about its molecular structure. If our eyes are considered as instruments for detecting the properties of physical objects which make them reflect light differently, they are very inefficient indeed. They are much less efficient than our ears; for there is a one–one correlation between the audible pitch of a sound and the frequency of the vibrations in the thing emitting the sound-waves which make us hear it; and we can, by hearing, distinguish different components of a complex sound-stimulus, e.g. those emitted by different musical instruments. In vision there is no one–one correlation between the colours we see and any physical property of the objects emitting or reflecting the light which makes us see them; and our eyes cannot distinguish the different components of a light-stimulus.

If any readers are still disposed to affirm Realism regarding colours, there are further difficulties for them to deal with. Here are a few.

(i) Realism concerning the colours which *we* see presupposes that the visual mechanism with which evolution has endowed (most) human beings *reveals* the inherent colours of things. Can this be defended in view of the varieties of visual mechanisms in other creatures?[15] Many of these respond to slices of the electromagnetic spectrum different from that which affects our eyes. Some creatures, e.g. bees, have four types of colour-receptor, and can presumably discriminate more colours than we can. Some, e.g. salmon, have three types of cone, but the wavelengths to which these are most responsive differ much less than those to which our cones are most responsive. Some creatures, including some colour-blind humans, have only two types of cone. And some creatures do with their ears what most do with their eyes. Thus nocturnal bats locate distant objects and identify them by sonic radar, i.e. by hearing echoes of sound-waves which they emit many octaves higher than any we can hear. Presumably such bats experience sense-data possessing qualities whose variations indicate the distances, shapes and sizes of the things which they perceive thereby. Presumably a Realist would not be so anthropocentric as to claim that it is only human sense-organs which reveal the qualities inherent in things. Then he seems to be committed to concluding that the bat's supersonic squeaks reveal things' secondary qualities which we are not equipped to discern.

(ii) A Realist concerning secondary qualities may think vaguely of colours, sounds, and odours, which exist out there, being transmitted to his mind via his brain. But can this way of thinking be defended? Does he really believe that *colours* are transmitted along the optic nerve, *sounds* along the auditory nerves, etc.? What travels along *all* our nerves are events of the same kind—series of pulses of electrical potential. The amplitude of the pulses is a constant for each nerve, and the only respect in which the 'message' conveyed by a nerve varies, is the rate at which the pulses succeed each other. The different kinds of sensible qualities which we experience depend, not on differences in the *nature* of what is transmitted from different sense-organs, but on the *places* in the brain where the pulses terminate.[16]

(iii) The pattern of light-waves which the tomato reflects is determined by its molecular structure. But its molecules are composed of atoms, and we are told that atoms are mostly empty space. Eddington has presented the physicists' account of the nature of a table by saying: 'Sparsely scattered in that emptiness are numerous electric charges rushing about with great speed; but their combined bulk amounts to less than a billionth of the bulk of the table itself.'[17] On this account, it cannot be the physical table which has the colours it looks nor the smooth texture which we feel when we touch it. The qualities of visual and tactual sense-data pervade *continuous* expanses. On the physicists' account, solid objects like tables are not really solid, and the stuff which composes them is almost as discontinuous as the so-called solid matter in a planetary system.

To sum up: the arguments expounded in this and the last chapters may not all be equally compelling. If one or two of them stood alone, a Realist might be excused for dismissing them, even if he cannot see how to answer them. But surely the combined weight of all these arguments is overwhelming. All of them indicate that no sense-data can be surfaces of physical objects, many of them that sense-data are fleeting by-products of cerebral processes. The arguments to show that secondary qualities are not properties inherent in physical things evidently require the same conclusions. For when one looks at a tomato, it is a *single* visible something which has the colour and the shape; so if the colour is in the observer, how could the shape be in something outside him?

Part Two

# A Defence of Common-sense Realism

# 4
# A Critical Survey of Alternative Theories

OUR defence of Realism will start with a critical survey of the main types of theory between which we seem obliged to choose if Realism is rejected. These theories will not be elaborated further than is necessary in order to recognize their more obvious weaknesses, and we need not explore variations on their themes.

## The Representative Theory of Perception

This theory is sometimes referred to as 'the Causal theory'. I shall avoid this term for two reasons. First, that it is sometimes interpreted in too weak a sense, as claiming only, for example, that 'our seeing what we do is causally dependent on the action of light from material objects'.[1] On this interpretation, the Causal theory is a truism. Secondly, the Causal theory is sometimes interpreted[2] as claiming primarily, or in part, either that our perceptual judgements involve making inferences as to the nature of the causes of our sense-data, or alternatively that our beliefs about physical things have been reached by making such inferences. The latter alternative, concerning as it does the development of the mind, is for psychologists to try to verify, if they can. Its verification presents obvious difficulties, for, if we all went through a stage of making such inferences, this was during a period of infancy beyond our recall. As adults, we make such inferences infrequently—only when observing unfamiliar objects, or familiar objects in conditions which are unfamiliar or not known at the time. Even a person subject to an illusion or hallucination rarely *infers* what he is seeing, hearing, or feeling; the nature of the object of which he is perceptually conscious is normally taken for granted.

The Representative theory makes a positive and a negative claim. The negative claim may be expressed thus: no sense-datum *is* (is identical with) a surface of a physical object; or, more generally, since the latter formulation is appropriate only for vision or touch: no sense-datum can literally be, or be part of, the physical thing or process to which one spontaneously attributes it. The positive thesis is that there are physical things, and that our sense-data *represent* the latter. And here "represent" should not be equated with "resemble", for those who accept the Representative theory almost always maintain that sense-data resemble the relevant physical things in some respects but not in others, that physical things should be conceived as literally possessing only the so-called primary qualities, but that even secondary qualities, those which belong only to our sense-data, do represent properties of physical things. For example, that though "green" and "red" refer to qualities which do not inhere in tomatoes, such qualities of certain sense-data represent certain physical properties of ripe and unripe tomatoes, and are thus reliable guides in selecting those which are fit to eat.

The basic objection to the Representative theory is that to adopt it is, in effect, to cut off the branch of the tree on which one is sitting. The theory implies that we could have no grounds for accepting it. If the negative thesis were true, the positive thesis would be unverifiable, for the negative thesis implies that we are never in a position to compare a physical thing with the sense-data which supposedly originate from it. Then we can never verify any statement about the resemblance, or lack of it, between sense-data and their physical sources. This consideration reveals incoherence not only within the theory but in using the arguments which are advanced to support it. The premises of these arguments include factual statements about physical things, e.g. about their real shapes, about mirrors, about amputation of a limb, about processes in the central nervous system, etc. Eliminate all such statements and the arguments cannot be formulated.

For anyone who accepts the negative thesis, the only consistent conclusion is surely that his sense-data are produced by unknown and unknowable causes. There is a celebrated passage in Locke's *Essay* where he seems to have been acknowledging this (2.2.23,

§§ 1–2). Having said that the idea of any specific type of 'substance', e.g. an orange or a table, includes 'the idea of substance in general', i.e. the idea of the *thing* in which its qualities inhere, Locke concludes that this idea is an idea of something we know not what, of an unknown support of 'qualities [i.e. powers] . . . capable of producing simple ideas in us'. By "simple ideas" he means sense-given qualities like whiteness or hardness. He presents this account not simply as a corollary of the Representative theory but as if it were, also, *our* idea of substance. He speaks of 'some substratum *wherein they* [sense-given qualities] *do subsist,* and *from which they do result*' (my italics), and glosses over the different implications of the italicized clauses. Moreover, having asked what colour inheres in, and answered: 'in solid extended parts', he asks what solidity inheres in. He has here evidently forgotten his thesis that the primary qualities of a body are 'inseparable from it', and overlooked the fact that the property of being solid *could* only inhere in a solid.

Though his argument was confused, Locke's conclusion was appropriate. Anyone who accepts the negative thesis of the Representative theory ought to conclude that the cause(s) of his sense-data are something(s) he knows not what. And this should presumably be applied not only to 'external objects' but to what he takes to be his own body. Locke forgot about this. But the arguments from phenomenal variability and hallucination apply to sense-data ascribed to one's own body, e.g. tactual sense-data, which one ascribes to one's skin as well as to external object(s) in contact with one's skin. The tactual sensation feels bigger when a penny is touched by the tongue than when it is touched by the palm of the hand, and the phantom limb hallucination is probably the best authenticated type of hallucination. The conclusion that ought to be drawn then is that my belief that my own body is a solid which has certain changing shapes is one which I cannot directly verify, one which I could only justify by problematic inferences. But this, surely, is a *reductio ad absurdum.* Presumably even a Realist would admit that, strictly speaking, all that sight and touch reveal of *external* bodies are parts of their surfaces. For however often you slice a tomato or a corpse, all that you can see or touch of it are more *surfaces.* But however strictly we speak, it is false to say this about one's own body. Though one's *tactual* sensations are located in parts of its surface, one is aware of the inside of this body, different regions of which are, from time to time, pervaded by sensations of various kinds—feelings of strain, pains, chills, glows, etc. For each of us, there is one body, his own, whose property of filling a volume is *sense*-given. But acquaintance, from the inside, with one such three-dimensional solid is enough to explain how we have each come by the idea in question, and why we attribute solidity, in this sense, to external objects. It is an explanation which Locke and many others have overlooked. The Representative theory should surely be dismissed on the ground that it implies that one is required to justify one's belief that one's own body is not spherical, and indeed that it is a solid of any shape and not merely a something one knows not what possessing the power to produce voluminous sense-data in oneself. And what could then be meant by "in", and by "oneself"?

The Representative theory has sometimes been defended by arguing that statements about the existence and nature of physical things are to be treated as hypotheses, and by outlining arguments whereby such hypotheses may be confirmed. The premises of such arguments have to include causal principles, notably (i) that everything must have a cause, and (ii) that for all differences in the effects, the sense-data, there must be corresponding differences in their causes. The first moves would be (*a*) that my sense-data are not caused by me, since, for example, what I see or hear is determined, at least in part, by factors not under my control; and (*b*) that my sense-data are not caused by each other since they are so fragmentary and disconnected. Often, for example, I hear a bark without having seen or touched or smelt a barker. My auditory sense-datum cannot then be explained as being caused by my other sense-data.

Arguments such as the following may then be developed:

(1) Visual and tactual sense-data are ordered in four dimensions, three spatial and one temporal. Therefore their unobservable causes must be similarly ordered.

(2) Whenever some visual or tactual sense-datum varies independently of its companions, e.g. a bulgy shape moves or grows smaller against an unchanging background, there must be some three-dimensional solid which is independent of those causing the sense-data which have not changed.

(3) That when we experience series of sense-data which vary in ways which are reversible, e.g. ranging in shape from a circle via

fat to thin ellipses *and then back to a circle,* there must be at least two independent cause-factors, one responsible for the variation and one for the 'common theme'; the common theme being attributable to the real shape of the unobservable cause, the variation to other factors. ("Common theme" is used here to refer to the similarity which obtains between the phenomenal shapes of a penny, and that which obtains between the phenomenal shapes of a postcard, but does not obtain between members of these two sets of shapes.)

It may be claimed that such arguments confirm the hypotheses that the unobservable causes of our sense-data comprise a plurality of independent things, and that many of these are three-dimensional solids which sometimes change and move, and so on. Such arguments may be elaborated further, but for our purpose this is unnecessary; for they cannot achieve their goal. What has to be explained is the fact that we *know* many facts about physical objects, including our own bodies. The sort of arguments outlined above could, at best, render such facts more or less probable. It is incongruous to present known facts as 'hypotheses'. Use of this word suggests that the Representative theory is being interpreted as an account of how we have *acquired* our knowledge, rather than of how we can justify it once sceptical doubts have been raised. In any case, there is a fatal objection to the causal arguments which we are considering. Suppose we grant the truth of their premises, the relevant causal principles and descriptions of our sense-data, we may infer only that the unobservable causes comprise a plurality of factors, but not that these are physical objects. This point may be made by means of an example used by Price.[3] The various shapes produced by someone trying to draw a circle may show a 'common theme', but here the factor responsible for their similarity is not a circular object, but an 'idea' in a person's mind. This, in effect, was Berkeley's answer to Locke, to which we must now turn. I shall follow the custom of describing Berkeley's theory as 'Idealism', though 'Ideaism' would be more appropriate.

## Berkeleian Idealism

This will be introduced by describing the reasoning which led Berkeley to what he regarded as being demonstrably the correct solution of the problems posed by Locke's theory. Berkeley's starting point was Locke's ontology, i.e. his beliefs about the irreducibly different types of entities in the universe. For Locke these were: minds, many finite and one infinite, the 'ideas' in each mind, and physical things. Berkeley decided that the last item must be deleted from Locke's list, and, in his *Principles of Human Knowledge,* he presented the following reasons for doing so:

(i) that Locke's assumption that physical things exist unperceived ('without the mind') is unverifiable;

(ii) that Locke's account of physical objects is unintelligible, since (*a*) no meaning has been, or can be, given to saying that an unknown something *supports* unknown qualities (or that the latter *inhere in* the former), and (*b*) causes must be active, and matter, according to Locke and the physicists, is 'inert' and so could not 'act upon spirit'.

(iii) that the only genuine, active, causes with which we are acquainted are mental acts, volitions, so the only intelligible answer to the question 'what causes my sense-data ('ideas of sense')?' is: the volitions of 'some other will or spirit'.

Sometimes Berkeley used terms of abuse when referring to matter as this was described by Locke, calling it 'senseless' and even 'stupid'! And sometimes he appealed to aesthetic considerations, as in his *Second Dialogue*: 'How vivid and radiant is the lustre of the fixed stars . . . Is not the whole system immense, beautiful and glorious beyond expression and beyond thought? . . . How should those principles be entertained, that lead us to think all the visible beauty of creation a false imaginary glare?' (Everyman edition, p. 244.)

The point which is usually presented as Berkeley's most decisive criticism of Locke—that the argument from phenomenal variability to prove that secondary qualities are mind-dependent applies with equal force to primary qualities—was waived by Berkeley in the *Principles*; all that this argument shows, he says, is 'that we do not know by *sense* which is the *true* extension or colour of an object'. Later, however, in his *Dialogues,* Berkeley invoked the argument from phenomenal variability to show that both primary and secondary qualities exist only 'in the mind', that they are qualities of sense-data ('ideas of sense').

Berkeley's main objections to the Representative theory were that it involves the duplication of objects, and that the supposed realm of inert objects was not only superfluous but unintelligible;

that the only objects that we want, need, or can conceive of, are the familiar things which have colours, tastes, smells, etc., and that such objects are 'collections of ideas'. Yet he claimed to be defending common sense, and said that what he was 'taking away' are not substances 'if the word . . . be taken in the vulgar sense', but only 'that which philosophers call matter'. Berkeley maintained that the role which philosophers had ascribed to physical things must be played by God; that God creates our sense-data without the aid of intermediaries and that the rules which He follows in doing so are what we call 'laws of nature'; and that since the things that we can see and touch are not always being perceived by any of *us*, what is meant by speaking of their 'continuous existence' must be that they are, at all times, being perceived by God.

So much for exposition. Readers will scarcely need help in recognizing paradoxes in Berkeley's claim to be defending the convictions of 'the vulgar'. Berkeley's central argument is that "exists", when it does not mean 'is perceiving', must mean 'is perceived'. The most surprising feature of Berkeley's *Principles* is his repeated claim that this point will be obvious to anyone who 'looks into his own thoughts', who considers what he means by "exists". If "idea" and "sensation" are used in their everyday senses, it is indeed clear that sensations do not exist without being experienced, and that ideas do not exist independently of being perceived—if "perceived" includes, as it did for Berkeley, being conceived or imagined. But, as Berkeley acknowledges, he was using "idea (of sense)" and "sensation" to refer to the things that we see and touch, eat, drink, and wear. Then it is plainly false that what we mean by saying that such things *exist* is that they are perceived. Notice the error in one of Berkeley's supporting arguments: that it is 'a manifest repugnancy' to claim that you conceive of something existing unconceived, since *you* are then conceiving what you suppose to exist unconceived. The error here is fairly obvious. Berkeley is confusing 'I conceive x without conceiving x' with 'I conceive *that* there are things of which I have not conceived'. The former is self-contradictory, but not the latter.

Berkeley's claim to be defending common sense can be criticized from many directions, but the chief complaints to be made concern his way of trying to accommodate the vulgar belief that things seen and touched are *publicly observable* and exist *continuously*. Berkeley's central argument, that *esse* is *percipi*, presupposes that my ideas exist only in *my* mind, yours only in *yours*. Then he seems to be committed to concluding, if he is alone in his study, that 'upon shutting my eyes, all the furniture in the room is reduced to nothing, and barely upon opening them it is again created'. In the *Principles,* Berkeley's answer to this objection is much less explicit than in the well-known rhyme, according to which

> . . . the tree
> Continues to be
> Since observed by yours faithfully, God.

Here he says only that there *may* be some other spirit which perceives things when we do not. His later writings[4] make clear, however, that he held that God *does* continuously perceive the things which we perceive intermittently or not at all, or at any rate that He perceives the 'archetypes' of these things. This way of interpreting the tenets of Realism involves extreme paradoxes. On Berkeley's account, the collection of sense-data which comprise a certain penny must include each of the distinguishable sense-data which any of us does or can sense in all possible conditions. Each of these sense-data is, according to Berkeley, a distinct idea. For Berkeley denies, in the Introduction to the *Principles,* that we can form 'abstract ideas'; and, on his account, a 'visible idea' would be abstract unless it had a *determinate* shape, a *determinate* size, and a *determinate* colouring. Try then to conceive the visual experience with which God is being credited. He must simultaneously sense *all* the visual sense-data which we could obtain from any viewpoint and under any conditions; and not only for this penny or that tree, but for every perceptible object in the universe, every mote of dust. Though our minds boggle at this suggestion, it may be said that this is because we, unlike God, are finite. But consider further the fact that Berkeley's God must be simultaneously perceiving all obtainable sense-data *of all species,* including tactual data and the kinds of sensations which we feel in regions of our bodies, twinges, sensations of muscular strain, erotic sensations, etc. Is it intelligible to credit an immaterial spirit with such omni-sentience when we consider the implications? Perhaps it was such considerations which led Berkeley to speak sometimes of the objects of God's continuous awareness, not as 'ideas' but as their 'archetypes'; meaning, presumably, God's thought of e.g. this tree, that is, of His rules for creating corresponding sense-data in us. (Then God must be credited with the ability to frame what Berkeley calls 'abstract ideas'.) But however we interpret his account of God's ideas, Berkeley is adopting a Representative theory. Whether God's idea of a certain tree is a certain infinite collection of His sense-data, or is His plan for producing in us now this, now that, member of such a collection, in either case the entity which *my* present sense-datum represents is *unobservable by me,* or by you. For Berkeley does not claim that God or his ideas, be these thoughts or sense-data, are perceptible by us. So Berkeley has not after all accommodated the common-sense view that physical things are immediately presented to our senses of sight and touch. God may perceive all of our 'ideas', but each of *us* can perceive only his own. In any case, it was illegitimate to present, as an account of what is believed by 'the vulgar', a theory of perception which requires belief in a God who plays the roles assigned to Him by Berkeley, or in any god.

## Phenomenalism

This is a natural development from Berkeley's theory; it is reached by subtracting God from his system. Indeed Berkeley seems occasionally to be advocating Phenomenalism, as when he says:

> The table I write on, I say, exists, that is, I see and feel it; *and if I were out of my study I should say it existed, meaning thereby that if I was in my study I might perceive it,* or that some other spirit actually does perceive it (*Principles,* III. My italics.)

> the question whether the earth moves or no, amounts in reality to no more than this, to wit, whether we have reason to conclude . . . *that if we were placed in . . . such or such a position and distance, both from the earth and sun, we should perceive the former to move among the choir of the planets . . .* (Ibid., LVIII. My italics.)

Phenomenalism is an extremely simple theory. It can be stated very briefly, either as an ontological thesis, i.e. about what exists, or as a linguistic thesis, i.e. about what we mean when we talk about physical things. On the former interpretation, it is the thesis that any physical thing *consists* solely of actual or possible sense-data. On the latter, it is the thesis that all that we *mean* by talking about any physical thing can be conveyed without loss by statements about actual or possible sense-data. The linguistic interpretation of Phenomenalism has been the commonest, at any rate during the last few decades. It is not, however, obvious why anyone should want to defend linguistic Phenomenalism unless he also accepts the corresponding ontological thesis. In so far as linguistic Phenomenalism claims to convey, not merely what we *do* mean, but what we *should* or *must* mean by our statements, it seems to presuppose the ontological thesis. In both formulations of Phenomenalism the phrase "possible sense-data" is used. This is not, of course, the name of a species of sense-data. It is a short way of referring to hypothetical statements of the form 'such and such sense-data would be sensed by . . ., *if* . . .'

Phenomenalism is an extreme application of Occam's Razor. All types of entities other than sense-data are dismissed as 'fictions' or 'logical constructions'. Phenomenalists could, and perhaps should, retain minds to be aware of, and to interpret, sense-data; but usually they have deemed minds to be a theoretical luxury, talk about which is to be analysed, like talk about tables, in terms of talk about sense-data. The ontological frugality of Phenomenalism is not its only attraction. It has been thought to be the only theory of perception consonant with the verification principle. This is a principle which has seemed self-evident to some philosophers; though they have not yet succeeded in so formulating it that it implies just what they want it to imply. It may be introduced, as it was by A. J. Ayer in 1936, by saying: 'a sentence is factually significant to any given person, if, and only if, he knows how to verify the proposition which it purports to express'.[5] Ayer went on to provide a very succinct proof of Phenomenalism:

> we replace the word "idea" in this usage [that of Locke and Berkeley] by the neutral word "sense-content"* which we shall use to refer to the immediate data not merely of "outer" but also of "introspective" sensation . . . we know that it must be possible to define material things in terms of sense-contents, because it is only by the occurrence of certain sense-contents that the existence of any material thing can ever be in the least degree verified. And thus we see that we have not to enquire whether a phenomenalist "theory of perception" or some other sort of theory is correct, but only what form of phenomenalist theory is correct. For the fact that all causal and representative theories of perception treat material things as if they were unobservable entities entitles us, as Berkeley saw, to rule them out *a priori*.[6]

* This was Ayer's 1936 synonym for "sense-datum", the term which he has used in his later writings.

Surprisingly, Ayer did not mention Realism as one of the rival theories which need to be eliminated. Presumably it then seemed obvious to him that his verification principle ruled out as meaningless some of the Realist's tenets, notably the existence of things whilst unperceived.

Phenomenalism may appear plausible at first sight; so long as we formulate it in very general terms, explain why it *must* be accepted and do not try to give the required translation of even a single sentence. This was Ayer's procedure in 1936, when he was content to say '"I am now sitting in front of a table" *can, in principle,* be translated into a sentence which does not mention tables [or himself?], but only sense-contents' (my italics).[7] The attempt to fulfil the programme leads, however, to endless complications. Even a statement as simple as Ayer's example concerning a table is intractable. Its translation into a sense-datum language would require an indefinite number of statements about sense-data obtainable from other places and by other people. If it is a *table*, and not, say, a reflection or a painting, it must be visible and tangible from many other places; and if it is not a hallucinatory or a dream table, it must be visible and tangible by other people. But how can a phenomenalist identify places and people *without referring to physical objects*? It would be frivolous to claim that any statement about a physical object is completely translatable into statements about actual and possible sense-data, if, in describing the latter, he must use if-clauses which mention other physical objects. Berkeley's translation of "the earth moves" referred to the earth and the sun. But the phenomenalist's programme requires that he should dispense, or at least explain how to dispense, with terms like "earth" and "sun".

Attempts have been made to meet this challenge. It cannot be met simply by describing sense-data which do in fact belong to a particular table, since there may elsewhere be other tables exactly like this one; so the location of the table in question must be identified. A proposed method for doing this is by describing the sense-data which I (or you or 'one') would obtain in moving to a viewpoint near the place in question. Now linguistic Phenomenalism claims to be analysing the *meanings* of *our* statements. In order to explain what is meant by "There are mountains on Mars", a phenomenalist would have to describe sense-data which the speaker or hearer or 'one' would sense *throughout* a journey to Mars, which seems preposterous. Our language provides simple devices for referring to individual objects, e.g. "Mars", "London", "the capital of England", "the cairn on Snowdon". A phenomenalist translation of a statement which uses any such expressions will have to substitute descriptions of imaginary sense-data obtainable by an imaginary traveller; and present these as part of what we meant in making the original statement! Even a translation of Ayer's statement about a table would have to describe imaginary journeys in order to identify other viewpoints. Moreover, the phenomenalist's description of what *we* call 'movements' or 'journeys' should not use any such words; for the notion of motion presupposes an enduring framework of three-dimensional solids located in a single space.* The imaginary journey to Mars, for example, would have to be described by the phenomenalist in a way which leaves it open whether the waxing size of a certain visual sense-datum is due to the imaginary observer approaching Mars, or to Mars approaching him, or to Mars growing in size!

Suppose, however, that a phenomenalist could succeed, by means of a pure sense-datum language, in identifying the desired location of the observer, and the direction in which he is then to point his eyes or his fingers, he still needs to add a crucial if-clause—if the observer sees or feels *what is there*. This way of putting it admittedly begs the question against Phenomenalism, by presupposing that any physical object which we can see or touch is there to be perceived, that it exists independently of being perceived; and this is something which the phenomenalist wishes to deny when he claims that all that we *mean* by saying that unperceived objects 'exist' is conveyed by hypothetical statements about sense-data. How then is he to translate into a pure sense-datum language the indispensable if-clause which we express by saying: if the observer perceives, notices, *what is there*?

Another serious objection to Phenomenalism may be expressed by saying that it implies that (actual) things or events are caused by unfulfilled possibilities. The oak-tree is supported by, and nourished via, its unseen roots. One's sense-data are causally dependent upon processes in one's brain. The references to unobserved roots and brain-processes are, on the phenomenalist's account, references to 'possible sense-data'; but that is just a short

* Strictly, we should, I think, say that physical space consists of the spatial relations between such solids.

way of referring to unspecified statements of the hypothetical form: '*if* . . ., then such and such sense-data would (or could) be obtained', and the possibility of formulating the requisite hypothetical statements is left as an unverified hypothesis. So it would be absurd to say that a tree is supported, or that your sense-experiences are caused, by unfulfilled possibilities. Hypothetical hypothetical statements are not entities of a kind which can be called cause-factors, and indeed are not *entities* at all. Ayer has tried to meet this criticism by legislating that "cause" and kindred words may properly be used only in statements made in 'the material object language', and not in the sense-datum language into which they are supposedly translatable. This is a desperate remedy. It would debar us from asking questions about the causes of sense-data which scientists do ask, and answer.

There are many other respects in which phenomenalists' analyses of what we mean (should mean?) by everyday statements depart radically from what we do mean by them. One more example will suffice. It is an axiom of Phenomenalism that sense-data are private, that a person's sense-datum is a datum only for him and is numerically different from any sense-datum sensed by another person, even when they are, as we say, hearing 'the same noise' or seeing 'the same star'. Our Realist conviction that physical things are publicly observable, that it is numerically the same noise or star which you and I perceive, has to be reinterpreted in terms of resemblances between the contents and/or the structure of sense-data sensed by different people. The *evidence* for such resemblances is that different people agree in their descriptions of what they see, hear, etc., on certain occasions. Let us waive the problems which arise if we try to justify passing from such evidence to conclusions concerning the resemblances between different people's sense-data. (These problems seem insuperable if we accept 'the' verification principle.) Assuming, as we all do, that there are such resemblances, *why should there be*? An answer is forthcoming if we accept (*a*) Realism, or (*b*) a Representative theory, or (*c*) Berkeleian Idealism: namely that when, for example, we look at the same object, our descriptions of what we see agree *because* (*a*) we see the same physical surface, or (*b*) our sense-data are caused by the same physical surface, or (*c*) our sense-data are produced by God in accordance with a particular idea in His mind. For a phenomenalist, however, *there is no answer*. It is just a brute fact that different 'streams of sense-data' are sometimes similar in content and/or structure, that they flow on *as if* their contents were caused by objects which are public and which continue to exist and to interact with each other whether they are being perceived or not. According to Phenomenalism, the order and regularities within each stream of sense-data, and the similarities between different streams, must be accepted with pious resignation as series of inexplicable miracles. If any reader is still tempted to flirt with Phenomenalism, let him try to give the required kind of translation of this statement, whose meaning is surely perfectly clear: for millions of years there were on this planet no sentient creatures, and therefore no sense-data.

## Sensibilism

This is a type of theory which has found few supporters. It was advocated by Russell in *Mysticism and Logic* (London, 1910); and was developed by Price in *Hume's Theory of the External World* (Oxford, 1940), as a theory towards which Hume's inconclusive discussion pointed. It deserves attention, however, for its intrinsic interest, and because it is an option liable to occur to anyone who has sought to render Phenomenalism intelligible. The phenomenalist conceives his desk as a collection, class, or family of sense-data. During much of its history the desk is unperceived and then this family has no actual members; and when it is perceived only a few members of the family cease to be merely possible. If the family is to have anything like the unity and continuity which we ascribe to the desk, the gaps between the (actual) sense-data need to be filled with something less insubstantial than hypothetical hypothetical statements. We need not fill the gaps, however, with somethings-we-know-not-what, for we can fill them with *unsensed sense-data*. But this expression is self-contradictory, if a sense-datum must, by definition, be sensed, and this is how "sense-datum" is normally used. To avoid confusion, we may introduce the term "sensibile" (that which can be sensed). Then we may say that a physical object is a family of sensibilia* some of which are, from time to time, sensed and are then called 'sense-data'. This solution conforms with Occam's Razor, for we are not postulating a new type of entity, but are merely attributing continuous existence to entities of which we are immediately aware; simply denying that *esse* is *percipi* in respect of things like patches of colour, cold

* "Sensibilia" is the plural of "sensibile".

expanses, etc. And the temptation to say of them that *esse* is *percipi* disappears when we stop describing them as 'ideas' or 'sensations', or as 'sense-data' meaning things which *are* sensed. On the present theory sensibilia are physical entities, in that they are constituents of physical things.

Notice that Sensibilism accommodates all of the tenets in terms of which I have defined "Realism", except perhaps the last—the ascription to physical objects of causal powers. However, even a Realist cannot (if he has read Hume) claim that causal powers are visible or tangible, and must admit that learning about the causal properties of things involves inferences of some kind. And the same may be said by a Sensibilist. The claim made by Phenomenalism to express what we (the vulgar) mean by our talk about physical things seems to be justified if it is made on behalf of Sensibilism. Then is Sensibilism not just a new terminology for expressing our common sense convictions? Why has it been presented as a novel and daring theory?

The answer is that Sensibilism has been advocated only by philosophers who were already convinced that Realism is untenable. Their reasons for rejecting Realism were not (or at least ought not to have been) the science-inspired arguments which, if valid, prove that sense-data are fleeting by-products of cerebral processes. They have presumably been convinced by the arguments from phenomenal variability and/or hallucinations. These arguments are thought to refute Realism by showing (i) that most sense-data cannot be what the Realist takes them to be, (ii) that considerations of resemblance and continuity require that the same goes for sense-data whose qualities coincide with the 'real' properties of physical objects. How then does Sensibilism deal with these arguments? It does so by claiming that *all* sense-data are equally real, are sensibilia which have an objective existence. The family of sensibilia comprising the penny has no privileged members; the black and elliptical sense-data and the brown and round sense-data have equal status as members of the family. This egalitarian principle does involve a departure from our common-sense ways of talking and thinking. Especially regarding hallucinations. Price was egalitarian about them too: the only short-coming of a hallucinatory sense-datum is the non-existence of the other sensibilia needed to enable it to live a normal family life. It may be wholly 'wild', i.e. have no siblings, or it may have only a few. A mirror-image was described by Price as an incomplete family—its members are spread out over a volume of space, but only on one side of the mirror.

But if these answers are given to the arguments against Realism expounded in chapter 2, Sensibilism must go further. A piece of paper viewed from the same place may successively look $_{(ph)}$ many different colours, depending upon the state of adaptation of the eyes, the media through which it is viewed, the nature of the illuminant, etc. The Sensibilist is obliged to say that each of these many different colours is a quality of the same physical surface, that it has each of these shades all the time and that which of them one sees depends on factors extraneous to the paper. The main objection to Sensibilism is now plain. It seems much too extravagant. We are being asked to believe that the same part of the same physical object simultaneously possesses incompatible qualities of the same genus. One of the few statements which nearly all contemporary philosophers would agree to be self-evident, though not obviously a tautology, is that the same surface cannot at the same time be wholly and uniformly pervaded by two different colours. The Sensibilist's answer to the argument from phenomenal variability requires rejection of this statement; and of many other common sense beliefs, e.g. that the same water cannot simultaneously be warm and cold.

This is true if Sensibilism is consistently applied. Russell, however, was not consistent. In *Mysticism and Logic,* where he used "appearances" and "sense-data" more or less interchangeably, he wrote:

> The appearance of a thing is a function of the matter composing the thing *and of the intervening matter.* The appearance of a thing is *altered* by smoke or mist, by blue spectacles or *by alterations in the sense-organs of the percipient* . . . (p. 165. My italics).

Russell does not here concede to science-inspired arguments the conclusion commonly claimed for them, that sense-data (appearances) are 'produced in us'; but he concedes enough to destroy Sensibilism. If we suppose that the qualities of a sensibile have been *altered* by processes in my sense-organs or central nervous system, what right have I to identify my sense-datum with the supposed sensibile? The latter becomes a something I know not what, for I am never in a position to compare a sensibile with a sense-datum which has not been 'processed' by my central nervous system. Sensibilism cannot afford to concede anything to the science-inspired arguments against Realism. It can then accommodate all the tenets of Realism. The trouble is that it commits us to much more than we want: to the reality of pink rats, ghosts, the persistence of limbs which have been amputated, etc.; to the conclusion that each part of a physical object permanently possesses incompatible qualities. Sensibilism might be described as Realism which has run riot. It bestows "real" so much more liberally than the Realism of common sense. If I had to choose between the theories of perception surveyed in this chapter, I should, however, choose Sensibilism. The other theories cannot accommodate some of the tenets of Realism.

It may help readers who have to take examinations if I summarize here what these other theories imply concerning the eight tenets of Realism. These tenets may be summarized as claims about perceptible physical objects, namely that these

(1) are located in physical space,
(2) are accessible to different sense-organs,
(3) are immediately presented to sight,
(4) are immediately presented to touch,
(5) are accessible to different observers,
(6) have a continuous existence,
(7) retain their perceptible properties when not being perceived,
(8) possess causal powers.

According to the Representative theory, tenets (3) and (4) are false, (7) is true for primary qualities but false for secondary qualities, and the other tenets are true; though, as we have seen, this theory makes all eight tenets unverifiable.

According to Berkeleian Idealism, tenet (1) is false, tenets (3) and (4) may be deemed true; but though Berkeley claimed that the other tenets are true, these would be true only on what we may call a very Irish interpretation thereof. There is, however, an ambivalence in Berkeley's thought—he tends to oscillate between the views of the vulgar and the viewpoint of the deity. If a table consisted of *our* sense-data, tenets (3) and (4) would be true, and tenet (2) could be defended on the ground that such a 'collection of ideas' comprises sense-data of different species (visual, tactual, etc.), but (5), (6), (7) and (8) would then be false. If a table consisted of

God's idea(s), and this seems to be Berkeley's considered opinion, then tenets (3) and (4), as well as (2) and (5), would be false, and (6), (7), and (8) though true would be unverifiable by us.

Phenomenalism claims that all eight tenets are true, but only (3) and (4) would be literally true; the others would be literally false, and true only in a very Irish sense.

My survey of the alternative theories of perception is not, of course, complete. Perhaps the most important omission is Kant's theory. It would be extremely difficult to do justice to this in short compass. Kant might be said to embrace a Representative theory, and to be the only philosopher who took it to its logical conclusion, namely that the entities of which appearances (sense-data) are appearances are wholly unknowable, and that we are not entitled to ascribe to them spatial *or even temporal* ordering. Indeed Kant went further: he claimed that we cannot apply the conception of causation to the unknowable things-in-themselves. He did not succeed in complying with his own rules, and anyone who did would be debarred from formulating any version of the Representative theory, which must say something about the hypothetical *causes* of our sense-experiences.

## 5

# A Critique of the Phenomenological Arguments

In chapter 2, the phenomenological arguments were classified according to the types of factors responsible for the phenomenal variations. As critical readers will have noticed, that classification presupposes the truth of some of the tenets of Realism: the continuous existence of physical objects, including human observers, in a single three-dimensional space, and the accessibility of such objects to different observers. It is surely impossible to formulate any of the arguments against Realism without using language which presupposes some of the tenets of Realism. We cannot, however, reinstate the Realism of common sense simply by making this point, for the tenets in question are also accepted by the Representative theory, yet the latter rejects other features of Realism, notably the tenets concerning the immediacy of vision and of touch, and the realist's beliefs about secondary qualities.

A brusque critique of the argument from phenomenal variability is given by G. J. Warnock in two short paragraphs of his book *Berkeley*.[1] He describes his target as 'the argument from illusion', and he equates this with a 'group of arguments [which] trades on the fact that objects sometimes seem different to different observers'. Though his criticisms are directed primarily against Berkeley's version of such arguments in his *Three Dialogues*, Warnock evidently thinks that they dispose of all versions thereof. He suggests that 'the argument from illusion' cannot get started unless one accepts something which he says Berkeley 'asserts', namely that 'if some property were 'really inherent' in an object, the object would necessarily *appear* to have that property in all circumstances'. Does Berkeley ever make such a statement?

Warnock gives no reference, but he may have been referring to a passage[2] where Berkeley is showing what he thinks follows from *Locke's* premises. Warnock describes as 'fantastic' the view which he attributes to Berkeley. He says that 'obviously an unusual light will alter the look of things', but that: 'To normal observers in ordinary daylight things *look* the colours that they really *are* . . . sugar *is* sweet because it tastes so to normal people.' He adds: 'The very fact that we say that people sometimes make *mistakes* implies that we know perfectly well how to decide what qualities things really have.'

Warnock's primary target was a thesis which he attributes to Berkeley—that all 'sensible qualities' are 'equally apparent'. Again, this was not Berkeley's view but one which, he argued, follows from Locke's premises. Berkeley's view was that all sensible qualities are equally real. His thought was that all sensible qualities inhere in 'ideas of sense' (sense-data) and not in Locke's somethings-we-know-not-what. However, if a philosopher argues from phenomenal variability *either* that all sensible qualities are apparent *or* that all are real, we are entitled to protest as follows:

(*a*) that he is rejecting our familiar distinction between the *real* and *apparent* colours or shapes or sizes of things, and that this distinction is indispensable for communicating about what we perceive;

(*b*) that this distinction is being rejected on the strength of arguments whose premises use this distinction, draw our attention to cases where the apparent properties of things differ from their real properties.

If Warnock's critique is reformulated thus, it seems to apply to the two-stage argument formulated in chapter 2 above, with reference to a penny. One of its premises is that the penny has a certain *real* shape, size and colouring. Yet the conclusion is that none of 'its' sensible qualities are real properties of the penny, implying, presumably, that they are all *apparent* properties. We seem to be entitled to dismiss this argument as incoherent. If anyone sought to avoid this criticism, as I have suggested Descartes might have done,* by saying 'I do not claim to know what are the real properties of the tower (the penny)', he has no right, as Warnock points out, to speak of making mistakes, of being deceived, about a thing's (real) properties. And this position is plainly untenable,

* p. 27 above.

since we all know how to apply our everyday distinction between a thing's real and its apparent colours, shapes, or sizes.

We should, however, be overstating our case if we suggested that philosophers who have judged the argument from phenomenal variability to be fatal to Realism have rejected our everyday distinction between real and apparent properties. Many such philosophers have drawn this distinction in a way which conforms with what Warnock says about things sometimes looking the colours they really are. For example, Russell does so[3] in *The Problems of Philosophy*: 'When, in ordinary life, we speak of *the* [the real] colour of the table, we only mean the sort of colour which it will seem to have to a normal spectator from an ordinary point of view under usual conditions of light.'[4] Russell went on to say that 'the other colours which appear under other conditions have just as good a right to be considered real'. Was he being inconsistent? I think not, but before we go further, it is necessary to distinguish several of the importantly different senses in which "real" is used in English.

In chapter VII of *Sense and Sensibilia,* Austin described *one* use of "real". He presents this as *the* use (p. 68), as if it were the only one. This is the usage involved in speaking of 'a (or the) real so and so', where so and so is 'a substantive', i.e. a noun or noun-phrase, e.g. "duck", "pound-note", "pearl" or "colour of her hair". The point of prefixing these substantives with "real" is to say: *not* a decoy or *not* a toy, *not* a forgery, *not* artificial, and *not* the colour it has been dyed. In another common use of "real", "so and so is real" means that so and so exists, and "unreal" means non-existent (fictitious or imaginary or hallucinatory,etc.). Philosophers have sometimes erred through arguing as if this, the existential use of "real", were its only use. Surprisingly Austin ignores it, and sometimes seems to confuse it with the use which preoccupied him. On one occasion he speaks of a 'real hallucination', but does not explain what "real" means here. What has been commonly overlooked by such philosophical exponents of English usage is that "real" has a role quite different from the previous two, when it is attached to an adjective describing a perceptible property and is contrasted with "apparent". Austin does mention this usage in passing: that in which 'the *real* colour of the thing is the colour it looks to a normal observer in conditions of normal or standard illumination' (p. 65). But he rejected this account of "the real colour of", failed to put anything in its place, and thereby missed the opportunity to distinguish this use of "real" from others. And this, of course, is a use of "real" which is most important when discussing what Austin professed to be discussing, perception.

Let us look again at the first stage of the argument based on the varying $\text{looks}_{(ph)}$ of the penny, and let us consider separately variations in shape, in colour, and in size. When, in the premise, the penny is said to have 'a single real shape', what is here meant by "real shape" is the shape the penny $\text{looks}_{(ph)}$ when viewed from some point normal to one of its flat surfaces. (Note that "normal to" here means 'perpendicular to'.) In that case it is a mere tautology to add that the shapes the penny $\text{looks}_{(ph)}$ from substantially different angles are not, in *this* sense of "real shape", its real shape. It is obviously invalid to infer from this that anything is not real in some *other* sense of "real", e.g. the existential sense. But this *is* the conclusion which is drawn from the argument in question. The conclusion that it is not the real penny (not really the penny) which is visibly elliptical from here is a disguised existential statement: that what *exists* in my field of view and is visibly elliptical is not the surface of the penny and must be something else. This conclusion is drawn as a result of failing to distinguish different uses of "real".

Now consider the premise that the penny has 'a single real colour'. What is meant here by "real colour" is, presumably, something like 'the colour it $\text{looks}_{(ph)}$ when seen by a normal observer in normal conditions'. Then the argument cannot show that what we call its 'apparent colours' are not real, in some different sense of "real". The premises of the argument leave it an open question whether what *exists* in one's field of view and is visibly shiny-white is 'really' the penny, is 'the real' penny, whether the sense-given colour is 'really inherent in' the penny.

Now consider the premise that the penny has 'a single real size'. This case is not parallel to the previous two. It would be absurd to suppose that what we mean here by "its real size" is 'the size it $\text{looks}_{(ph)}$ under normal, or under any specified, conditions.' "Penny-sized" is not the name of a specific sense-given quality like "black" or "round". We do not have, nor could we find any use for, a convention which equated 'the real size' of a thing with the size it $\text{looks}_{(ph)}$ from a specified distance.* What we mean by speaking of the real size of a physical object involves size-relations be-

* The prisoners enchained in Plato's cave might have adopted such a convention. See *Republic*, Book VII.

tween it, in its different dimensions, and some arbitrarily chosen physical object, e.g. the standard metre which is kept in Paris. The argument from phenomenal variability would seem and be preposterous if it were based solely upon variations in the sense-given sizes of things. There is, however, an important sense in which sense-given sizes are measurable. The sense-given width of an object is the *angle* between the directions, from here, of its right and left boundaries, and so on. The sense-given size of a thing, where there is no distorting medium, is a linear function of its distance; which is a way of saying that if the distance between the object and the viewpoint is increased by any number N, the sense-given width and height will each be reduced by 1/N. I mentioned in chapter 2 Price's variant of the argument from phenomenal variability, concerning 'perspectival distortion'. This argument was disposed of by Price in a later publication.[5] As Price pointed out, variation in the sense-given (the 'field of view') sizes of a thing explains, since it entails, variation in its sense-given shapes. For when the square table-top looks$_{(ph)}$ trapezoid (i.e. none of its sides parallel), this is because its more distant edge(s) have, *from here*, a smaller field-of-view length than its nearer edge(s).

I have examined at some length the first stage of the argument from phenomenal variability, because it has been so widely accepted and so often discussed. We must not forget the second stage, which is needed to cap the case against Realism: the arguments that there is no 'intrinsic difference' between, and that there is a 'sensibly continuous transition' between, sense-data which do and those which do not have qualities which coincide with the 'real' qualities of the physical object perceived thereby. These arguments are far from being compelling when we formulate their principles in general terms. It is being assumed that if two things of which one is aware are entities of different natures, they must be 'intrinsically different', i.e. must have some detectable qualitative difference; and that they could not be members of a series in which there is a sensibly continuous transition between them. These principles are not at all self-evident. There is a sensibly continuous transition between what I see when I look at a lighted lamp and the elongated streak of changing shapes which I see with my eyelashes touching. Am I thereby committed to saying either that both visible objects are private or that both are public? Surely not. The arguments used at stage two are persuasive only if one has been convinced by stage one that most visual sense-data cannot be surfaces of physical objects.

All that I have done so far is to show that both stages of one of the commonest arguments against Realism are invalid; but I have only considered phenomenal variations due to changes in viewpoint or the relative position of the illuminant. Can the counter-argument which I have used be generalized to cover phenomenal variability due to factors of all other kinds? It is tempting to take Warnock's short-cut, to define "the real property of a thing" in terms of how the thing looks$_{(ph)}$ or feels$_{(ph)}$, etc., to a *normal* observer in *normal* conditions. But then a critic of Realism could protest thus:

(*a*) The case against Realism hinges not only on variability of the apparent$_{(ph)}$ properties of a thing, but in some cases on the *multiplication* of sense-data; and being a pair of things cannot be a property of *one* thing.

(*b*) The repeated use of "normal" in the proposed short-cut sounds soothing, but "normal" is not here being used in its normal sense. When "normal" is not used to express approval, it usually means 'usual'. And it is not unusual to see coins looking$_{(ph)}$ elliptical, or mountains looking$_{(ph)}$ blue.

(*c*) If a Realist who appeals to our everyday use of "real (versus "apparent") property" offers an account of this which mentions *each* of the conditions which he needs to exclude as not 'normal', he would end up with a very long and heterogeneous list. It would have to contain lots of qualifications, like 'not seen through optical instruments *except when these are needed to correct one's vision*'. It would be very implausible to claim that all the conditions which a Realist needs to exclude as not 'normal' are incorporated in Everyman's use of "real" versus "apparent".

Answering the last two points will be postponed until we have considered separately the remaining arguments presented in chapter 2. Let us start with double vision, which Austin described as 'a baffling abnormality'. We have seen why double vision might be considered to pose a unique and intractable problem for a Realist. The two sense-data 'of' the bottle are indistinguishable in quality,* they are sensed in different directions, and there is no possible ground for choosing *one* of them as (really) the bottle's

* Unless the double vision is induced by pressing one eye-ball, which makes one of the (sets of) sense-data blurred.

front surface. But surely a Realist should not be baffled about double vision, *if* he has noticed that it is a normal, though rarely noticed, concomitant of seeing. When one's eyes are focused on one's finger-tip, nearly everything else in one's visual field is duplicated. This is simply a consequence of the fact that we have two eyes in different places. It would be baffling if creatures with two such eyes, capable of variable depth of focus, did not experience such double vision. What ought to be found baffling, or at least marvellous, is the feat performed by the brain in somehow fusing two different views into a single view, seen from a place seemingly equidistant from each eye. If you inspect a matchbox about nine inches from your nose, you see it as a *single* solid of a determinate three-dimensional shape, and you can simultaneously see *four* of its faces; but if you pay phenomenological heed to them, two very different shapes are visible, and a face of the box visible to one eye is invisible to the other. Double vision does, however, oblige a Realist to complicate his account of the perspectival, the field-of-view, shapes of things. It is not enough to say, as Price did in 1956, that from a person's viewpoint (singular), a physical object has *the* field-of-view shape which it projects at that point (singular). *Two* viewpoints are involved in double vision. Moreover, when, with eyes focused on finger-tip, I see a steeple in two widely different directions, these two directions need to be specified by saying, not merely 'one from each eye', but also 'one relative to the direction in which each eye is looking'. But need more be said?

About mirror-images, a Realist may give a short answer: that seeing a reflection of the cat *is seeing the cat*, is seeing it not *in* or *behind* the mirror, but *via* the mirror. If English had provided an appropriate preposition, indicating the route by which something is seen, would English-speaking philosophers have been tempted to enlist mirrors in the anti-Realist cause? A well-designed language could also immunize us against the Bent Stick argument, by providing a preposition to indicate that something is being seen through two media like air and water whose adjoining surfaces bend light-waves. That the sense-datum is bent is consistent with its being the front surface of the stick seen *partly through* air *and partly through* air *and* water.

Do optical instruments raise any further problems for a Realist? Their effects on what we see are simply explained in terms of the laws of refraction which explain the bent stick phenomenon.

Admittedly they show that it is somewhat arbitrary to legislate about the meaning of "real shape or texture". We usually picture a thing as having the shape or shapes that it usually looks when viewed with the naked eye. But an object which we usually view, or can only see, through a microscope will be pictured as having the shape(s) and texture(s) which it then looks. The argument based on the variability of the sense-data resulting from the use of magnifying instruments would be embarrassing for a Realist *if* the shapes seen with and without such instruments are really incompatible. But are they? Surely the property of being smooth to the naked eye (and to touch) is compatible with that of being corrugated at the scale revealed by a microscope. If you say 'this surface is really smooth', and I say 'It's really corrugated', our statements are compatible if you mean, by "really", 'at the scale disclosed by the naked eye', and I mean, by "really", 'at the scale disclosed by such and such magnification'. Surely both uses of "the real shape of the surface" are legitimate, so long as they are not confused.

A type of case still to be considered is where sense-given qualities vary as a result of the state of adaptation of the sense-organs or the brain. Locke's example of water which feels warm to one hand and cold to the other has bothered Realists because the thermal qualities which we feel are normally described (and, by the unreflective, thought of) as qualities of environmental objects, e.g. water or ice or the air in the room. But a Realist need not, and, I suggest, should not here think with the vulgar. Regarding Locke's example, is it not obvious, on reflection, that the thermal qualities are felt *in one's hands*. This does not, however, require us to deny that the felt warmth and coolness are 'inherent in' physical objects; they inhere in two regions of the same physical organism, the observer's body. There is no inconsistency in the facts: that one hand is now sensibly pervaded by warmth and the other by coolness, and that these different sensible qualities are both caused by contact between liquid, all of which is at the same temperature, and hands which had become adapted to liquids at different temperatures. Notice that it is very common for us to speak of external objects having properties which we should all agree on reflection are not *theirs*. We sometimes attribute sadness to landscapes, to sounds, or to a drooping flower. We are then projecting on to external things feelings which they invoke *in us*. Flavours may be dealt with as I have dealt with thermal qualities. Guinness from the same barrel yesterday tasted quite sweet but now tastes like cascara. A Realist can accept the conclusion that such varying taste-qualities do not 'inhere in' the Guinness, without denying that they do inhere in physical objects, namely people's palates.

It may seem difficult to deal with our outstanding problem as brusquely as we have dealt with the others. Variation of phenomenal colours, due to adaptation, drugs, or jaundice, can scarcely be dealt with by a Realist as we have dealt with thermal and taste qualities. One of the tenets in terms of which I have defined "Realism" implies that the visible properties of things inhere in them. To treat its visible colour as being projected on to the tomato would be a drastic revision of Realism, and would presumably be repugnant to philosophers who wish to defend common sense. Moreover, this move would apparently drive us into the arms of one of the rival theories. For, if it is not the tomato which is visibly red, the red object in my visual field must be an entity of another type, a sense-datum in a sense which is *not* theory-neutral. Two suitably brusque arguments are available, however, to dispose of our present problem. The first was used by Price in *Hume's Theory of the External World*. It is that the empirical evidence only requires us to admit 'that some sense-impressions [sense-data] are dependent on the nervous system in respect of *some* of their qualities' (p. 108). Price adds that a few sense-impressions are dependent on the nervous system in respect of all of their qualities; but here he is referring to after-images which a Realist should refuse to classify as sense-data, and to hallucinations, which I shall discuss later. The second argument is Warnock's:

> if the conditions, or the observer's sense-organs, are abnormal, *of course* things will seem to be other than they really are. Of course a colour-blind man makes mistakes about colours; . . . Such cases are very familiar and not in the least disconcerting.[6]

Need more be said?*

The short-comings of Warnock's short-cut may now be discussed. This short-cut involved reminding us that our everyday use of "real (versus "apparent") property" is to be defined in terms of how things normally look$_{(ph)}$ or feel$_{(ph)}$, etc. One objection to this is that when we consider what has to be excluded as not normal, "normal" is being used abnormally. This complaint can be met,

* This question is not rhetorical.

however, by dispensing with the word "normal". Admittedly a penny is not usually seen from a direction in which it looks$_{(ph)}$ round. The point to be made here is that it is our convention to describe as 'the real shape' of a flat surface, the shape it looks$_{(ph)}$ from a direction perpendicular to that surface; and that this is not an arbitrary convention. Consider the difficulties which would confront us if we tried to adopt any alternative convention. We commonly speak of a penny or a table being round. This might be criticized as careless talk. For "round", unless it means spherical, is not the name of a three-dimensional shape. The physical shape of a penny is, roughly, that of a flat cylinder. It would not, however, be practicable to use "the real shape of a thing" in this way. Think of the host of shape-adjectives which we should then need in order to classify roughly the 3-D shapes of things like trees or tables. There is, however, some degree of freedom in choosing conventions for using "real shape", as we have seen in discussing what we see through microscopes. Or again, astronauts might adopt a new convention for using "seeing the real shape of a country". Only to them has America looked$_{(ph)}$ the 2-D shape shown on maps.

Regarding the colours of things which we describe as their 'real' colours, the use of "normal" in defining this use of "real" is, as we have seen, open to criticism. The critic might add that, in formulating our everyday convention for using "the real colour", it is not enough to say, like Warnock, 'to normal observers in ordinary daylight'. In direct sunlight, the shadowed side of a ball looks$_{(ph)}$ a very different shade from the rest of it, and if the ball is at all shiny, the part reflecting sunlight looks bright or white. A uniformly coloured surface looks$_{(ph)}$ uniform in colour in daylight only if the latter is diffused, e.g. under a cloudy sky. Many more qualifications would have to be made if we are to speak with any precision. However, precision of this kind would be misplaced if our aim is that of linguistic philosophers, namely to remind us about our everyday uses of words. For this purpose, it seems sufficient to say that "the real colour of X" nearly always means: the colour X looks (not looks$_{(ph)}$, since in everyday talk "looks" and "looks$_{(ph)}$" are not distinguished) when

X is viewed with the naked eye,
the only medium is transparent, e.g. air or water,
X is at fairly close quarters,
X is illuminated by daylight.

These conditions, the last two admittedly rather vague, may be called conventions. But surely they are not arbitrary, for the conditions mentioned are those which maximize our ability to discriminate the colours of things; and so may be called 'the optimal conditions for recognizing things' colours'. Moreover, the colour a thing looks$_{(ph)}$ under these optimal conditions enables us to predict how it will look$_{(ph)}$ under other conditions, e.g. at a greater distance or through fog, whereas the converse is not true.

A critic may point out that the optimal conditions for recognizing a thing's shape do not coincide with the optimal conditions for recognizing its colour(s). This is true. At the height from which one could see the shape of the British Isles, one could not discriminate the colours of the flora. All this shows is that we need not follow philosophers who speak too generally of the 'real properties of things' being 'perceived in normal conditions'. Each sense-organ has its own kind of optimal conditions. And for sight, we need to distinguish the optimal conditions for shape-perception from those for colour-perception. It is not our convention that the real colour of a surface is the colour it looks$_{(ph)}$ from a direction perpendicular to that surface. And there are different optimal conditions for seeing the shapes of very large objects, of very small objects, and of what Austin called 'moderate sized specimens of dry goods'. What such considerations show is that "real", in the sense which now concerns us, performs somewhat different roles in different contexts; like "real" in the sense which preoccupied Austin, which may mean: not a toy, not a fake, or not a peroxide blonde.

The argument from hallucination must now be considered. This argument gapes with large holes. The form of the argument is this. There are cases where hallucinatory sense-data are indistinguishable from 'normal' sense-data, therefore both must be entities of the same nature; that since hallucinatory sense-data are, by definition, not surfaces of physical objects, the same goes for 'normal' sense-data. This argument relies upon the same shaky principle as the second stage of our first argument from phenomenal variability: the assumption that if two objects of consciousness are indistinguishable, they must be entities of the same nature or 'category', e.g. both physical or both mental. But how could this assumption be justified? Consider the various objects of consciousness which we call 'mental images': the pictures in the mind's eye which accompany remembering or imagining, and after-images and dream-images. We do not consider that these are entities of the same nature as things seen and touched in normal waking consciousness, if "of the same nature" means, as it must in the present argument, having the same kind of existence, being the same kind of thing. Yet some mental images are 'of the same nature' as the objects of normal perceptual experience in another sense: that they have the same kinds of sensible qualities, e.g. colours and field of view sizes. We must refuse to follow philosophers like Moore who so define "sense-datum" that it applies to a mental image. We all believe that *esse* is *percipi* in the case of mental images. The Realist view is that *esse* is not *percipi* in the case of sense-data, that to talk about 'visual and tactual sense-data' is a way of talking about the parts of independently existing objects which are present to our senses.

When we consider the testimony which is cited to support the factual premise of the argument from hallucination, the best that can be done to establish it is to report cases where a person *does* mistake a hallucinatory object for a physical object. But to argue from 'not distinguished' to 'indistinguishable' always goes beyond the evidence. Were people who have reported hallucinations ever, at the time, in a critical, phenomenological, frame of mind? Were they looking for respects in which what they took to be normal perception might differ from the latter? There is no evidence that they were in cases culled from psychical research or hypnosis experiments. We may then suppose that these people mistook unusually vivid mental images for sense-data. We are liable to mistake such images for sense-data. An after-image may be taken for a stain or shadow on the wall-paper, so-called spots before the eyes may be taken for unidentified distant objects. Psychologists tell us that some people have short-term memory images ('eidetic images') so stable and distinct that they can discover therein features of recently seen objects which had not then been noticed. And dream-images may be very vivid. Larkin's reported encounter with the absent M'Connel may have been a dream—he may have dozed off before the fire.

Regarding hypnotically induced hallucinations, some psychologists argue that because subjects talk and act as if they see what they have been told to see, we need not assume that there are *any* corresponding objects in their visual fields.[7] Orne's experiment described in chapter 2 above suggests that hypnotized subjects do at least *see* something, but this something could be a vivid image. That this is so is indeed suggested by one of the experiments in which Orne compared the reactions of hypnotized and 'faking' subjects. Subjects of each type were told that they would see a person sitting in a chair which was in fact empty. The hypnotized subjects commonly, the faking subjects never, said things like 'This is very peculiar, I can see Joe sitting in the chair and can see the chair through him.' This suggests that the hypnotized subjects did at least see an image of Joe, but also that it was simply a mental image which they would have recognized as such if they had been in anything like a normally critical frame of mind. This reinforces the point that 'not distinguished' does not warrant 'indistinguishable'.

Regarding the phantom limb hallucination, pains are very commonly reported, and sometimes sensations which may be called 'tactual', e.g. itches and tickles. It is, however, unjustifiable to draw conclusions about tactual sensations in general. Realism need not, and, as I have defined it, does not, take any stand concerning the status of pains. If the facts force us to conclude that pain-qualities are generated by the brain and 'projected' into other regions of the body, we need not reject any of the Realist's tenets about perception. Pains are not indispensable for perceiving one's own body; and the same goes for itches and tickles. For them, like pains, *esse* is *percipi*. What would be really embarrassing for a Realist would be if people reported having in an amputated hand, tactual sensations indistinguishable from those involved in discriminating by touch, e.g. cricket balls and hockey balls, polished and unpolished wood. But this, so far as I know, has never been claimed.

Philosophers who use the argument from hallucination may complain that I am setting an unreasonable standard in requiring *proof* that other people's hallucinatory data are indistinguishable from their normal sense-data. To this we may reply that it is also unreasonable to ask *us* to abandon Realism and accept one of the paradoxical alternative theories on the strength of reports of experiences of kinds which *we* have never had. Before a philosopher accepts the factual premise of the argument from hallucination, surely he should at least try to obtain some relevant experiences. He need not sacrifice a limb if he is hypnotizable. Unfortunately I am not.

## 6

## A Critique of the Science-inspired Arguments

WE may start by protesting against the uncritical use by Locke and others of the phrase "produced in us". To speak thus of sense-data begs the question against Realism and glosses over some of the main problems implicit in rival theories. Normally when we speak of things being 'produced', we mean that they are assembled or synthesized out of pre-existing things or materials. But if our sense-data are produced by patterns of electrical activity in our brains, "produced" must mean *created*. Our sense-data have qualities (e.g. colours and flavours) which are not possessed by the relevant brain-processes. Sense-data are not produced *out of*, not made *of*, brain-processes or brain-cells, in the sense in which omelettes are made of eggs, or water of hydrogen and oxygen. So the kind of production which is involved is the kind with which God is credited in creating the Universe. But why create a mystery involving the continuous creation of sense-data, when there is a simple alternative at hand; namely that the function of the relevant processes in the central nervous system (CNS) is, not to create private entities, but to reveal, disclose, acquaint us with, public objects? A Realist need not question the findings of physicists and physiologists concerning the causes of perception. Nor need he bother about the details, since nobody now believes that the sensible qualities of the tomato *travel through* one's sense-organs and afferent nerves. All he need insist on is that the function of the relevant physical processes is, not to create fleeting private entities, but to disclose durable physical objects, including the percipient's body. We must not confuse the mechanisms on which perception is causally dependent with the objects which we do perceive.

Need more be said? Unfortunately it must. Some philosophers who have rejected Realism have not simply ignored the view just outlined. C. D. Broad has considered and rejected it, calling it 'the Selective theory of perception'.[1] H. H. Price and R. J. Hirst have also rejected this theory, and have adopted what Broad had called 'the Generative theory', namely that sense-data are created by processes in the CNS. However, what each of these philosophers called 'the Selective theory' was not given a fair hearing. Price introduced this theory towards the end of his critique of Realism;[2] at a stage when he had already concluded that sense-data must be fleeting products of cerebral processes. The only alternatives which Price considered, concerning the function of processes in the CNS, are (*a*) that these generate sense-data or (*b*) that they reveal, selectively, certain pre-existing sensibilia. Price equated 'the Selective theory' with Sensibilism, and in his first book he rejects this theory for reasons similar to those given above in chapter 4. Hirst[3] follows Price's reasoning on this issue. But what needs to be considered is an alliance between the Selective theory and Realism, or rather the fact that a Selective theory is already presupposed by the Realism of common sense, and our everyday uses of language. The kind of Selective theory of which this is true is the modest thesis that the function of processes in the CNS is to reveal some of the physical things which are there and some of their properties. Unfortunately this modest thesis has been ignored by the philosophers who have used the term "Selective theory". They used it to refer to the extravagant thesis that every obtainable sense-datum exists permanently, waiting to be sensed if and when 'selected' by appropriate processes in the CNS of a suitably placed observer. I shall use "the Selective theory" to refer to the modest thesis which is presupposed by our everyday uses of verbs like "see". It is only in the following innocuous senses that a Realist should describe perception as *selective*:

(*a*) that we can select what we see, touch, hear, etc., by controlling our movements;

(*b*) that we can select which perceptible properties of objects, or which qualities of sense-data, we discriminate, by controlling our attention;

(*c*) that the sensory apparatus with which we are endowed is selective in the sense that it discloses only *some* of the things around us (not e.g. bacteria) and only *some* of their properties (not e.g. their reflectance of ultra-violet waves).

The last point indicates how a Realist may meet arguments based on differences between the sense-organs of different species. Nobody has qualms about concluding from their behaviour that dogs smell smells which we cannot. Nor need we have qualms about supposing that there are colours which the eyes of bees enable them to see, but which we cannot. My situation relative to that of the bees is presumably that of colour-blind people to me. The 2 per cent of us (males) who have only two types of cone are unable to discriminate colours as conspicuously different (for others) as red, yellow, green, and brown. Even if 98 per cent of us suffered from this kind of colour-blindness, they would still have grounds for calling themselves "colour-blind". The majority would be able to infer that there must be some colours which they cannot see, seeing which enables the minority to discriminate consistently between things indistinguishable in colour to them (the majority). They could confirm this by simple experiments, whether or not the minority introduced, for their own use, colour-names which the majority could not consistently apply by using their own eyes. The rhetorical argument about bats which was used in chapter 3 need not disturb a Realist. For surely only a very naïve Realist could think that the qualities of the sounds which it makes inhere in a trumpet, in the sense in which its visible shape and colour inhere in it. But if we do not treat the sounds which we hear as being literally *in* the objects from which they originate, why should we put ourselves between the bat's ears and do this on the bat's behalf?

One of the science-inspired arguments against Realism does require some revision of our common-sense assumptions—the time-lag argument. That sounds take time to travel is obvious from everyday experience. That the same goes for light only became clear in the light of astronomer's measurements and some recherché experiments. It comes as a shock when one first realizes that the sun is not in the direction in which one sees it. But we can easily adjust our thinking without abandoning Realism. We may say that we see things as they were, and where they were, at an earlier time, and this will apply to the defunct star as well as to the sun. The difference in date is negligible and can be ignored except when we are looking at celestial bodies.

It has been claimed that sense-data have been artificially produced by electrical stimulation of the brain, or alternatively, that the facts in question show that the distinction between sense-data and mental images dissolves. A philosopher ought not to accept such conclusions on evidence which is fourth-hand (or third-hand if he has read the experimenters' reports). The patients are said by the experimenters to say that they never interpret the artificially induced sensations as perception of external things. This undermines the case for classifying these sensations as sense-data rather than as images. And Penfield's account of what the patients say about the 'flash-back' experiences is too brief to enable us to decide that their contents may not be classified as mental images, whether their owners would have done so if they had been quizzed about this. Let us, however, concede as conceivable that in future one could oneself be made, by direct interference with one's brain, to have hallucinatory experiences which one believes at the time to be genuine perception, even perhaps of hearing a symphony and seeing Barbirolli conducting the orchestra. Should we then be *obliged* to conclude that all that we ever experience are sense-data *qua* fleeting products of cerebral processes? Surely not; for this conclusion would be based on the principle that objects of consciousness which are indistinguishable must be entities of the same nature or 'category'. And this principle, as we have seen, is not self-evident. Nor is it even true, since, for example, a real (externally caused) noise may be indistinguishable from a singing in one's ears.

Consider now the thesis that some of the perceptible properties of things, the so-called secondary qualities, are not *their* qualities at all. Suspicions are aroused by the changes in the properties assigned by scientists to this class. Until early in the twentieth century solidity and impenetrability were excluded, but are now included in this class, and indeed the only properties currently excluded by physicists are too abstract to be called sensible qualities, e.g. mass and electrical charge. We are now asked to believe, not only that the table is not really coloured, but that it is not really solid. L. S. Stebbing has forcibly criticized physicists for saying such things. Provoked by Eddington's statement that a table or a plank 'has no solidity of substance', she wrote:

> What are we to understand by "solidity"? Unless we do understand it we cannot understand what the denial of solidity to the plank amounts

to. But we can understand "solidity" only if we can truly say that the plank is solid. For "solid" just is the word we use to describe a certain respect in which a plank of wood resembles a block of marble, a piece of paper, and a cricket ball, and in which each of these differs from a sponge, from the interior of a soap-bubble, and from the holes in a net . . . The point is that the common usage of language enables us to attribute a meaning to the phrase "a solid plank"; but there is no common usage of language that provides a meaning for the word "solid" [such] that [it] would make sense to say that the plank on which I stand is not *solid* . . . If the plank appears to be *solid*, but is really *non-solid*, what does "solid" mean? If "solid" has no assignable meaning, then "non-solid" is also without sense. If the plank is non-solid, then where can we find an example to show what "solid" means?[4]

A physicist might find this argument unconvincing. He might invite us to his laboratory to witness experiments showing that various 'fundamental particles' pass through planks without making holes in them, and might say: there is my example to show what "non-solid" means, namely penetrable by particles of matter. Perhaps Stebbing would have retorted that the physicist is giving a new meaning to "solid", and that its not being solid in this sense is compatible with the plank's being solid in our everyday sense; and indeed that Eddington's description of his table as 'mostly emptiness' presupposes that the table is solid in the everyday sense, that it fills a determinate volume of space. For Eddington tells us that the 'combined bulk' of the electrical charges therein 'amounts to less than a billionth of *the bulk of the table itself*'. And what could the last phrase mean if it does not refer to the table which visibly and tangibly occupies a certain region of space?

Stebbing dealt much more briefly with the thesis that colours exist only in us, that they are, in Eddington's phrase, 'mere mind-spinning'. She simply says:

the *rose* is coloured, the *table* is coloured, the *curtains* are coloured. How, then, can that which is not coloured duplicate the rose, the curtains, the table? To say that an electro-magnetic wave-length is coloured would be as nonsensical as to say that symmetry is coloured. Eddington does not say so. But he has failed to realise that a coloured object could be *duplicated* only by something with regard to which it would not be meaningless to say that it was coloured.[5]

This argument is, I think, too brief and blunt, but it can be developed as follows. Colour-words are items in *public* languages;

we communicate information by using them. How did we learn to use such words? The obvious answer is that we were taught their meanings by having our attention drawn to exemplars, e.g. to ripe tomatoes, British pillar boxes, etc., by someone who pronounced "red", until the association between the word and the colour was established for the learner. Unless the resembling hues of ripe tomatoes, human blood, etc., were publicly observable qualities of such things, we could never have been taught to use "red" as we do. Unless we postulate 'innate ideas'; but in the present context this would have absurd implications. We should have to suppose that babes born of English-speaking parents have a built-in association between red shades and "red", while French babes have a built-in association between reds and "rouge", and so on round the world. Colours must be publicly observable properties of things, since this is a necessary condition of a state of affairs which exists, i.e. that people communicate about colours. A ripe tomato is a paradigm case of a red physical object. "Red" and "physical object" are given the meanings which they have by our using them to refer to such things. In view of this 'no ripe tomatoes are red' *cannot* be true. The science-inspired arguments which have led people to draw such conclusions *must* be fallacious. The argument just expounded is put more pithily by Gilbert Ryle:

> Secondary Quality adjectives are used and are used only for the reporting of publicly ascertainable facts about common objects; for it is a publicly ascertainable fact about a field that it is green, that it would look so and so to anyone in a position to see it properly. What else could the people who teach other people to talk, teach them about the use of these adjectives?[6]

The science-inspired arguments against Realism are based on the assumption that the physical sciences discover not only how physical things behave, and what they are made of, but also *what they are really like*. This assumption is a natural one to make, or at least it was so long as the unobservable entities postulated by such sciences were described in ways which are intelligible. But nowadays, though physicists still talk of 'fundamental particles', they describe the latter in ways which preclude their being particles. We are told that an electron can get from one place or orbit to another without passing through the intervening space; that an electron sometimes travels backwards *through time* and then forwards again; that light behaves both in ways which preclude its consisting of particles and require us to conceive of it as a wave-front *and* in ways which preclude its being a wave-front and require us to conceive of it as consisting of discrete particles, photons. So the physicists admit, and often stress, that we can no longer conceive of such entities as particles, or indeed picture them at all. What is more serious, however, is that the behaviour attributed to the ultimate constituents of matter precludes us from conceiving of them as particulars, as individual entities which retain their identity through time. What could be meant by saying that *the same* physical something occupies different places, if we abandon the requirements (i) that if 'it' does so at different times, 'it' must travel through the intervening space, and (ii) that 'it' cannot *simultaneously* occupy *different* places? The latter requirement is violated by saying that an electron travels backwards and then forwards in time, since it implies that there are moments when 'it' is simultaneously in different places. Then what on earth could be meant by "the same electron", the hypothetical traveller? We are told that it is physically impossible to determine the precise location of an electron at a given moment, because trying to do this would interfere with and alter what one is trying to detect. This is intelligible. But the conclusion which has been drawn by many physicists is that an electron *cannot have* determinate spatio-temporal locations. And this has led some of them to talk about 'probability-waves' as if the latter were entities. But unless the probabilities in question are probabilities *that* this or that electron *has* this or that spatio-temporal location (which we are told it cannot have), what on earth can "probability" *mean* here?

To the layman, microphysics appears to be in such a state of theoretical chaos that it is impossible to concede to it any authority to tell us what physical things are really like. A few philosophers would still concede this authority to physics. But an obvious position for a Realist philosopher to adopt is that the unobservable entities postulated by physicists are fictions of a sophisticated kind; that such fictions are useful and perhaps indispensable for guiding the scientist's imagination, leading him to formulate new laws or hypotheses which he can then proceed to test; but that the scientist's real subject-matter is the behaviour of *observable* physical objects: tables and planets, geiger-counters and oscilloscopes, etc. The *observable* properties and behaviour of such things provide the scientist's starting point, and also his terminus, in that it is by observing them that his laws and theories must be tested. The view which I have just outlined is described by J. J. C. Smart as 'Phenomenalism about sub-microscopic objects'. It could be expressed as a linguistic thesis by saying that scientific statements about unobservables are (or should be) translatable into statements about observable objects or processes. I have formulated it as an ontological thesis: as the denial that the 'fundamental particles' of current physics are real, are the constituents of which tables, planets, and ourselves are composed. The contrary view is defended, by Smart, and he calls it 'Scientific Realism'.[7]

Phenomenalism about sub-miscroscopic entities seems to be the obvious position for a common-sense Realist to adopt, in view of the incoherence of the things that physicists currently say about such entities. And there is also much in classical physics which invites this interpretation. Forces and fields have often been spoken of as if they had physical reality; but this is gratuitous. Newton's laws of motion describe how *observable* bodies *do* move. The symbol in his equations representing 'the force of gravity' need not be thought to denote anything like invisible elastic. (It was attributed by Newton to the variable elasticity of 'the ether'.) More obviously, the 'lines of force' which are depicted as radiating from a magnet need not be regarded as more than a device for depicting e.g. the directions in which its needle will point if we move a compass nearby.

The case for adopting Phenomenalism regarding the unobservables postulated by physicists has been stressed because this would dispose of the temptation to argue that physical objects are not really coloured, on the ground that 'fundamental particles', whether singly or structured in molecules, could not be coloured. If we accept Phenomenalism regarding such unobservables, it is incongruous to complain that our eyes are inefficient instruments for detecting the molecular structures which determine which patterns of light-waves are reflected. If molecular structure is a fiction, a useful pictorial symbolism for explaining how observable objects behave, it is absurd to complain that we cannot *see* the actors in the scientists' stories. In any case, even if one adopts what Smart calls 'Scientific Realism', it is inept to compare our eyes adversely with spectroscopes. Spectroscopic eyes would bewilder us with detailed information which would be useless (unless we had graduated in physics), but would not give us the indispensable information which our eyes provide, concerning the shapes, sizes and distances of many surrounding objects—and about their colours. Unless physical objects displayed various colours (including neutral colours), they would not be visible. Whether or not we agree with Bradley's dictum that 'without secondary quality, extension is not *con*ceivable', it is obvious that without secondary qualities, extended objects would not be *per*ceivable.

But does the Realism of common sense, which is what we are defending, require us to reject Scientific Realism, that is, to dismiss as a kind of mythology the atomic theory of matter? To concede this would, I think, be to weaken considerably, and unnecessarily, the case for common sense. Its kind of Realism does not involve acceptance of 'the' verification principle, according to which it is meaningless to postulate any entities which cannot in principle be experienced by us; requiring us, therefore, to 'reduce' all statements purporting to be about such entities to statements about our actual or possible sense-data. Common-sense Realism is clearly compatible with the view that our sense-organs are selective in disclosing only *some* of the types of things which exist, and only *some* of their properties. The atomic theory of matter is intelligible as an account of things which we not only do not, but could not, perceive. (If light-waves alias photons were visible to us, we could see nothing else.) In any case, the atomic theory ceased to be a hypothesis, as it had been since the days of Democritus, when John Dalton found how to verify it, namely by experimentally determining the combining weights of different elements, types of atom.[8]

Those who ask us to believe that the unobservables invoked in scientific theories are convenient fictions are asking us, as Smart puts it, to believe in 'a cosmic coincidence'.[9] One of our chief criticisms of Phenomenalism was that it makes miraculous the order found within each stream of sense-data and the correlations between the contents of different streams. There is a similar and equally powerful argument against a wholesale rejection of Scientific Realism. This rejection would imply that it is by sheer coincidence that observable objects behave *as if* composed of molecules, which are composed of atoms, which are composed of electrons, etc. The scope of the coincidence becomes incredible when we consider the extent to which predictions based on the atomic theory are fulfilled in detail: new poisons are synthesized and used to pollute our planet, nuclear bombs made and exploded, geiger-counters click on *as if* being struck by particles, cloud-chambers display tracks *as if* traversed by particles, etc., etc. The atomic theory does not *explain* any of these occurrences unless we interpret it as factual and not fictional. On the convenient fiction thesis, *there are* no atoms, etc., and it is an inexplicable miracle that the atomic theory fits the host of empirical facts which it was developed to explain and which it has led us to discover.

Surely common-sense Realism must somehow be reconciled with Scientific Realism. This is one of the main tasks for contemporary philosophy and one of the most difficult. It cannot be tackled here, beyond making very briefly some points which seem important. Fortunately we are not obliged to accept as factually true either *everything* that scientists say, or *nothing* that they say, about their unobservables. A philosopher may, and I think should, adopt it as a principle not to accept on authority statements which he cannot understand and to reject statements which involve contradictions. On this principle he may accept the atomic theory as developed and used in chemistry, and the account of light-waves as used in optics and the theory of colour vision, while not accepting many of the statements made in microphysics. As they are currently described (and new species are being reported almost daily), so-called fundamental particles cannot be assigned any ontological status, since the descriptions of them involve contradictions. Microphysics is evidently awaiting its Newton. With these qualifications, however, Scientific Realism seems to be compatible with common-sense Realism, provided that the Scientific Realist concedes a point which I made earlier: that the behaviour of *observable* things provides the starting point, and the terminus and test for scientific theories. Surely it is a corollary of this that it would be inconsistent to interpret such theories as showing that *observable* things are unreal, or less real, than the entities invoked to explain *their* behaviour. This, I suggest, is the appropriate *short* answer to Russell's epigrammatic argument; 'Naïve realism leads to physics, and physics, if true, shows that naïve realism is false. Therefore naïve realism, if true, is false; therefore it is false.'[10]

# 7
# A Critique of 'the' Sense-datum Language

IN this chapter I try to get to the roots of some influential errors. The arguments become less simple as the chapter progresses. If or when beginners find themselves out of their depth, they can pass on to the next chapter, though not perhaps without some loss. I shall try to show: (*a*) that it is inappropriate to speak of 'the' sense-datum language since philosophers who use "sense-datum" or some synonym do not agree about the rules for its use; (*b*) that sense-datum languages are parasitic upon, and could not replace, languages in which we talk about publicly observable things; (*c*) that philosophers have adopted rules for using "sense-datum" which rule out Realism and that this is a result of their giving priority to the Cartesian quest for incorrigible statements; (*d*) that the rules adopted for the latter purpose defeat this purpose and also defeat the purposes for which philosophers have wanted to get incorrigible statements; (*e*) that A. J. Ayer's attempt to defend what he calls 'the sense-datum theory' against J. L. Austin's criticisms are not successful. I shall start, however, by noting an important step forward taken by Ayer in his *Foundations of Empirical Knowledge* (1940).

Previously philosophers who used "sense-datum" or some synonym had written as if they had discovered entities of an unfamiliar type. They introduced "sense-datum" with the help of a few simple examples, e.g. the thing whose existence you cannot doubt when you glance at a tomato, or what is actually seen when you look at a postcard; and then said no more about "sense-datum", but proceeded to describe the *objects* so christened. Descriptions of sense-data were presented in much the same style as Darwin's description of the fauna of the Galapagos Islands. In 1940 Ayer's approach was very different, presumably as a result of an important paper by George Paul.[1] Ayer argued in chapter 1 that it is inappropriate to ask whether 'the theory of sense-data' or 'the theory of naïve realism' is true, that 'these so-called theories of perception are not theories at all in any ordinary sense', since all empirical facts can be accommodated by each and no experiment could eliminate either; that the so-called theories are simply alternative languages for describing the same facts, alternative 'proposals to use words in a certain fashion'. Accordingly Ayer reformulated Phenomenalism. He wrote:

> If we cannot produce the required translations of sentences referring to material things into sentences referring to sense-data, the reason is not that it is untrue that "to say anything about a material thing is always to say something about sense-data", but only that one's references to material things are vague in their application to phenomena and that the series of sense-data that they may be understood to specify are composed of infinite sets of terms (p. 242).

Ayer recognized that if one introduces a technical terminology one has to *decide* what rules to adopt therein. His own rules for using "sense-datum", and the reasons he gave for adopting them, draw attention to the arbitrariness of the rules which had been covertly introduced by earlier philosophers. Consider some examples from H. H. Price's account of 'the nature of sense-data' in *Perception* (1932):

(1) that a sense-datum cannot exist unsensed (p. 113);
(2) that when one blinks, on opening one's eyes a *new* sense-datum 'comes into being, exactly like the old perhaps' (p. 113);
(3) that sense-data cannot be said to change (pp. 115–16);*
(4) that all of the qualities of a sense-datum are determinate, 'perfectly specific', and that 'terms like 'vague', 'definite' and 'indefinite' can be applied only to our cognitive acts' and not to a sense-datum (pp. 149–50).
(5) that 'the unity of a sense-datum—that which makes it *a* sense-datum . . . depends in part upon . . . the 'meaning' which the

* Price does not affirm this rule dogmatically, but he usually adopts it in theory, if not always in practice.

sense-datum has for us', e.g. 'when we look at a black and white cat, we sense one single sense-datum which is black in one part and white in another' (pp. 114 and 116).

Treated as pieces of natural history these claims are very surprising. Even when they are recognized as rules for the use of "sense-datum", they seem arbitrary and in need of justification. Price adopted rules (1) and (2) because he held that certain science-inspired arguments show that sense-data are fleeting products of cerebral processes. But how could rules (3) and (4) be justified? Rule (3) would commit us to saying that whenever a person sees something moving or changing in any respect, he is sensing a series of distinct sense-data, each of them infinitesimally different from its predecessor in direction or in quality. A technical terminology which observed this rule would be unusable. Philosophers who profess to adopt rule (3) normally proceed in practice to speak of sense-data moving or changing. But then they are conceiving a sense-datum as we conceive a physical object, i.e. as something which remains identical while its properties change; are thinking of a sense-datum as a substance, whose life-history is, however, much shorter than that of a mayfly. Rule (4) would commit us to denying, for example, that the shape of a visual sense-datum is ever 'vague' or 'indefinite'—as if the contents of one's visual field always had sharp boundaries! If we tried to observe this rule, how should we translate into a sense-datum language descriptions of the shapes we see when we look at smoke, shadows, mist patches and things seen through mist or through spectacles which make them look blurred?

Rule (5) seems to be least open to criticism, at first sight. It is, however, a way of glossing over one of the most serious problems in designing rules for a sense-datum language: how are we to identify *a* sense-datum, what are to be the rules for using "the same sense-datum"? This problem has two aspects: (*a*) we have to decide which elements in a visual field, or which of the simultaneous sounds that one can discriminate, are to count as different sense-data; (*b*) if we abandon the unusable rule (3), we have to decide when a present sense-datum is the same as, is a continuation of, an earlier sense-datum. Price's rule offers an answer to each question, but one which makes reference to physical objects indispensable. Yet Price introduced his investigation as being phenomenological (p. 10), and he had earlier described such an investigation thus: 'We must do our best to forget everything that we know or believe about physical objects, and we must resist the temptation to "refer" our data to such objects.'[2] Price was not trying very hard to do this when he identified *a* black-and-white sense-datum by ascribing it to a cat. His difficulty is, however, obvious. Without reference to the cat, he would have had to describe two or more sense-data whose specific shapes have no names and could only be conveyed by drawing them. Consider the difficulties in describing, without words which refer to physical objects, your visual sense-data when you are in the middle of a wood. Price's rule avoids such difficulties—but only by letting you count as *one* sense-datum almost anything you please —whatever is seen *as* one thing or pattern, e.g. each tree, or each branch, or each leaf, or each group of diverse things that you see *as* a group, or indeed the whole vista if you adopt an aesthetic attitude and view it as a whole, a gestalt. Regarding the identity through time of a sense-datum, Price's rule (5) is usually easy to apply when one is looking at what are recognized as physical objects. Then we can talk, as Price sometimes does, of the cat sense-datum prolonging itself on to the mouse sense-datum. But how is one to apply rule (5) in describing the sense-data experienced in looking at e.g. flickering flames, reflections in ruffled water, a firework display, etc.?

The sort of questions that I have raised regarding rule (5) led Ayer to say in 1956 that 'there can be as many [sense-data] as I choose to distinguish', that 'the notion of a sense-datum is not precise. Moreover, it appears to borrow what little precision it has from the way in which we talk about physical objects . . . It is, in fact, only by the use of expressions which refer to the perception of physical objects that we have given any meaning to talking of sense-data at all.'[3] Yet Ayer went on to say that it is 'a contingent fact' that 'we are all brought up to understand a form of language in which the perception of physical objects is treated as the standard case'; and that it is 'not inconceivable that there should be a language in which sense-experiences were described by the use of purely qualitative expressions which carried no reference to the appearances of physical object' (p. 123). Can these claims be defended? A creator of the kind of language which Ayer here envisaged would have to recapture the innocence of a new-born babe uninfluenced by knowledge about physical objects, but would have to invent a vocabulary adequate to describe the almost infinite varieties of sense-given shapes, colours, sounds, etc. Moreover, it may be argued* that a language is, by definition, a public institution, a vehicle for communication, and that the so-called language which Ayer envisaged would not qualify as a language, on the ground that its function would be to describe features of one's own sense-data, sense-data being, on Ayer's premises, private entities; and that if a person could invent such a 'private language', he could not convey to anyone else what he said in it. This argument, may, and I think, should, be challenged,[4] but it is superfluous. For it is not a *contingent* fact that we were brought up to use a material object language. We humans can only be taught to use words by having our attention directed to *publicly observable things* as exemplars of what the words are used to refer to or describe. How could we be taught to talk except by teachers applying expressions to things observable by their pupils as well as by themselves? It seems clear that learning a material-object language must come first; that any language in which 'sense-experiences were described by the use of purely qualitative expressions' must be parasitic upon a language which is *public*; public both in the sense that its conventions are common knowledge and in the sense that it is used to talk about publicly observable things.

This does not show, however, that a sense-datum language is impossible or useless. The language of mathematics must in practice be introduced by means of a material-object language, and it cannot be used to describe everything. Granted that a sense-datum language is in these respects like that of mathematics, we must ask whether it is philosophically useful. But then we must ask: useful for what? The chief complaint to be made here is that philosophers who have used "sense-datum" (or some synonym) have used it to serve two different purposes and have failed to recognize that their different goals conflict. Both of these purposes were mentioned in chapter 1 of this book:

First, the need for a terminology for giving phenomenal descriptions which are theory-neutral, i.e. which enable us to debate the arguments for and against rival theories of perception without begging questions or prejudicing the outcome.

Second, the Cartesian quest for indubitable statements to provide foundation stones upon which the edifice of human knowledge can be (re)constructed.

* And this has been argued by philosophers influenced by Wittgenstein.

Philosophers who use "sense-datum" have taken it for granted without discussion that these requirements coincide, that sense-datum statements meet both. Thus Ayer wrote in 1940: ' "the theory of sense-data" does not involve more than the elaboration of a special terminology for describing our perceptual experience. It must not be regarded as presupposing the validity of any particular theory either about the causes or about the character of what we perceive or sense'.[5] Yet he also wrote that 'if one uses a sentence such as "this is green" merely to designate a present sense-datum, then no proposition is being asserted to the truth of which any further evidence would be relevant', so that such statements could be said 'to be indubitable on the ground that it was not significant to say that one doubted them in any other but a purely verbal sense'.[6] The 'purely verbal' kind of doubt to which Ayer here refers is merely doubt as to whether one has, by a slip of tongue or pen, produced e.g. "green" when one meant "red".

Ayer adopted in *The Foundations of Empirical Knowledge* rules designed to achieve the goal of formulating statements which, barring verbal slips, are incorrigible; rules which, however, far from being theory-neutral, rule out Realism and preclude any visual sense-datum from *being* a surface of a physical object. Consider some of the rules which Ayer adopted:

(1) that we may not say that sense-data 'really have properties that they do not appear to have' (pp. 117–18 and 129–34);

(2) that we may not say that sense-data 'appear to have properties that they do not really have' (pp. 117–18 and 118–24);

(3) that we may not speak of sense-data 'whose existence is not noticed at the time that they are sensed' (pp. 117–18 and 125–8). Ayer combines rules (1) and (2) by saying: 'If one knows what properties a sense-datum appears to have, one knows what properties it really has' (p. 134). His way of formulating his rules was, I think, unfortunate. He attaches to "sense-datum" the expressions "appears to have . . ." and "really has . . ." Should he not rather have legislated that these expressions, and the distinction between 'real' and 'apparent' properties, are to be used only in the material-object language? Surely his rules need to be expressed differently if they are to serve his purpose of describing the relationship between what he is treating as alternative languages. Let us use "M" to represent any material object, "S" to represent a sense-datum which 'belongs' to M, and "P" to represent any perceptible

property. Then the rules which Ayer intended to formulate should presumably be expressed thus:

(1) A person's S does not have any P which M, or an apparent M,* does not appear$_{(ph)}$ to him to have.
(2) A person's S has any P which M, or an apparent M,* does appear$_{(ph)}$ to him to have.
(3) A person does not sense S unless he notices M, or an apparent M.*

In that case, each of the rules (1) and (2) rules out Realism. Applying rule (1)—sometimes we say that the moon 'looks cold'; but the moon does not look$_{(ph)}$ cold (or warm) for thermal qualities are not *visible*, so the visual sense-datum cannot *be* a physical surface possessing properties accessible to other sense-organs, including thermal qualities. Applying rule (2)—the moon looks$_{(ph)}$ flat, so the sense-datum *is* flat and cannot therefore be, as common sense assumes, the curved irregular surface of the moon. No philosopher whose aim is to give phenomenal descriptions in theory-neutral language should adopt rules (1) or (2). If Realism is not to be outlawed by linguistic legislation, we must leave open the possibilities that S may have properties which M does not now appear$_{(ph)}$ to have, and that S need not have all the properties which M does now appear$_{(ph)}$ to have. Realists who use "sense-datum" ought surely so to use it that "My sense-datum of M is so and so" means *no more and no less* than either 'M appears$_{(ph)}$ so and so to me' or 'There appears to me to be an M which appears$_{(ph)}$ so and so.'

Philosophers who use a sense-datum language have disagreed about some of Ayer's rules. These have been debated at length, and in such debates philosophers have usually followed Ayer's way of formulating such rules. Rule (1) has been rejected by Broad and Price. Consider their reasons. Broad wrote:

> We must distinguish between failing to notice what is present in an object and "noticing" what is not present in an object. The former presents no special difficulty. There may well be in any object much which is too minute or obscure for us to recognise distinctly . . . Consequently, there is no difficulty whatsoever in supposing that sensa† may be much

* The phrase "or an apparent M" is included to cover cases of illusion or hallucination.

† Broad's synonym for "sense-data".

more differentiated than we think them to be, and that two sensa may really differ in quality when we think that they are exactly alike.[7]

Price objects to rule (1) on the ground that it implies that a sense-datum might have 'a roundish shape, but not any definite *sort* of roundish shape'. To illustrate the implications of this rule, he writes: 'My sense-datum at first is just brightly coloured. *What* colour . . . ? No definite colour at all since I have not yet attended to that part of my visual field. But now I do attend, and the sense-datum *acquires* a more and more definite colour. It becomes first bluish, then blue-grey, then smoke-colour.' Price points out that it is perfectly good sense to say *of a flower* 'It did in fact *look* sky-blue, but I only noticed that it was bluish.'[8] In giving their reasons for rejecting rule (1), Broad and Price forgot the quest for the indubitable and were concerned with phenomenology; but both illustrated their arguments by referring to perception of material things: the minute parts of a (presumably physical) object, and a flower. In arguing against rule (1), they remind us that we talk, and think, of physical objects as having minute parts, or determinate perceptible properties, whether these are noticed or not. They do not, however, acknowledge as a reason for talking similarly about 'sense-data' that, if rule (1) is adopted, the sense-datum language is not theory-neutral.

Though they rejected rule (1), Broad and Price never questioned rule (2). And as we have seen, rule (2) by itself rules out Realism. At any rate it does so, if it is interpreted as I have suggested that it should be: i.e. as ruling that a person's S has any P which M appears$_{(ph)}$ to him to have. But we must now note that this interpretation is much too generous. Nowhere in *The Foundations of Empirical Knowledge* does Ayer distinguish phenomenological from other uses of such verbs as "appears" and "looks"; and in the passage where Ayer offers his reasons for adopting rule (2), he *confuses* their phenomenological use with their other main use, i.e. for giving estimates of the physical properties of perceived objects. Ayer alludes to what psychologists call 'shape-constancy', 'size constancy', etc. On the strength of what unidentified psychologists had said, Ayer asserts:

> Though philosophers seem inclined to assume that a round object, when it is seen obliquely, always *looks* elliptical, *the empirical fact is* that it usually does not. If I look sideways at a coin, the image that it projects

upon my retina is indeed elliptical, but in spite of that, the coin still *seems to me to be* round (p. 119; my italics).

The empirical fact which Ayer here misdescribes is that "It looks round" and "It looks elliptical" are compatible when, in the latter, "looks" is used in the phenomenological sense, and in the former means 'it seems to me *to be*'. One can simultaneously recognize an object as a round hoop and notice that it looks$_{(ph)}$ elliptical. Ayer had followed the psychologists who, when discussing 'shape-constancy', 'size-constancy', etc., had confused the very different tasks which may be set for the subjects: estimating the *real* properties of physical things, and describing how they *look*$_{(ph)}$. In 1940, Ayer used "looks", "appears *to be*" and "seems *to be*" interchangeably both in introducing "sense-datum" in chapter 1, and in specifying the rules for its use in chapter 2. This was, for his purpose, disastrous, since it makes the properties of sense-data not the hardest of hard facts, but the softest and most pliable. What Ayer's rule (2) amounts to is that when anyone says that something looks or appears so and so, whatever he says goes. Ayer accepted it as an 'empirical fact' that the penny looks round to me, if I say it does, from whatever angle I view it *and whatever I may mean by "looks"*!

Ayer's rule (3) excludes 'the possibility of there being sense-data whose existence is not noticed at the time' (p. 125). This seems innocuous, but some users of "sense-datum" have rejected it. Broad did so[9] on the grounds that one sometimes fails to see something which one is looking for and which has been 'staring one in the face'; and that it is natural to conclude that 'there was an undiscriminated, and at the time probably undiscriminable, sensum in my visual field'. On the other hand, A. M. Quinton has suggested[10] that our willingness to speak, in everyday language, of 'unnoticed experiences' is an unnecessary convention, that 'one could equally well, or better, opt for the other alternative and speak, not of 'unnoticed', but of 'possible experiences' ', i.e. of those which one would have had *if* one had been in 'the phenomenological frame of mind'. I think not. I am commonly incapable of remembering *anything* about the clothing of people to whom I have just been talking. I am certain that on such occasions I had been seeing their clothes, that I should have noticed if they had been naked or invisible below the neck. And surely it would be inappropriate to suggest that noticing what one has not noticed requires one to get into 'the phenomenological frame of mind'. That phrase loses its usefulness if it is to be applied whenever I do notice someone's dress. To say that people see only what they notice is an arbitrary restriction on "see". To restrict "sense-datum" to what is noticed is also arbitrary. Still it seems harmless, in that a sense-datum language which adopts this rule is theory-neutral. Yet adoption of rule (3) creates a problem. All users of "sense-datum" have made it a rule that all perception involves sensing sense-data. As some users of "sense-datum" have recently recognized, this term needs to be defined in terms of the phenomenological use of "looks", "appears", etc. But this implies that it is relatively rare for perception to involve the sensing of sense-data, since phenomenal attention is the exception rather than the rule. How is this conflict between the rules to be resolved? The simplest remedy is to reject rule (3), to say that when a person is awake he is always sensing sense-data, which he *can* notice, but usually does not. To use "sense-datum" in this way removes the temptation to reject Realism, since "sense-datum" is then just a way of describing how things look$_{(ph)}$, etc., when one does pay phenomenological heed. If this solution is not adopted, how else can we remove the conflict in the rules which we are considering? It would be disastrous to revert to using "sense-datum" in a way which ignores the differences between "looks" and "looks$_{(ph)}$". The kind of confusion which has resulted from ignoring this distinction may be illustrated by reference to an argument which has had considerable influence.

In *Perception*, Price made phenomenalism appear much more plausible than ever before. Earlier philosophers had claimed that a physical object (or its representation) is a *collection* of ideas or a *class* of sense-data. Price's substitute, 'a family of sense-data', was not merely a verbal change. He described the structure of the family in much more detail than had been attempted before. According to Price, all other members of such a family have their places in series, each of which radiates from a member of a certain set of sense-data —those which *constitute* the surfaces of the physical object. The more remote members of such series are progressively more distorted, by perspective, by the medium, perhaps by mirrors, and so on. The set which constitutes the surfaces of the object comprises only visual and tactual sense-data. Consider what Price says about the relevant set of visual sense-data: that it has 'a remarkable property . . . that ALL the members of it *fit together to form a single solid*' (p. 218; my capitals; his italics). These 'constructible' sense-data are christened 'nuclear sense-data', and we are told that nuclear sense-data are those obtainable within the range of perfectly stereoscopic vision. Price divides visual sense-data into three classes—perfectly stereoscopic, imperfectly stereoscopic, and those which are not stereoscopic at all. The last are flat, two-dimensional. Price makes the following claims for perfectly stereoscopic sense-data:

(*a*) 'the size and shape of the datum are independent of the direction in which it sensibly faces. Thus if I look at a match-box on the table just in front of me, two or even three* surfaces of it are present to my senses at once. I am acquainted with two (or three) sense-data belonging to it, which face in sensibly different directions; but in spite of this *they are all sensibly rectangular*' (pp. 218–19; my italics).

(*b*) 'within the zone of perfect stereoscopy there is no increase of sensible size with decrease of depth . . .' (p. 220).

(*c*) 'The nearer one stands to the thing, the larger the sense-datum, *until one reaches the* [*sc.* perfectly] *stereoscopic zone*' (p. 222; my italics).

Regarding the range of perfect stereoscopy, we are told only that 'the upper limit is probably only a few feet, the lower some six inches' (p. 219).

So Price is claiming that when you look at a match-box located within six inches to 'a few feet' of your nose, *all* the sense-data 'fit together', as the sides of the match-box would if they had been separated. He claims this on the ground that the sense-datum 'of' each side never changes in size or in shape when the box is within the critical range, regardless of the angles from which its several sides are viewed. Once the box gets beyond the critical range, then, but only then, do the sense-data 'of' its sides cease to be rectangular, and only then do they start to dwindle in size in proportion to their distance! If this was intended as phenomenological description, it is astonishing. "Rectangular" *means* being a four-sided figure each of whose angles *is a right angle*. How did Price fail to notice that none of the sense-given angles is a right angle when

* If Price had noticed that *four* sides of a match-box can be simultaneously seen, he could have avoided using some unconvincing arguments. (See pp. 241–3.)

two or three sides of the box are visible? And that the sense-data do wax in size as the box is moved from arm's length towards one's nose? The explanation is that he has switched from asking how things look$_{(ph)}$ to asking how they look, i.e. seem, or are seen, *to be*. Price was observing the box under conditions which made it most difficult to discount what he knew, and could see, to be its real shape and size, i.e. using both eyes at very short range. Even so, I find it surprising that he did not notice the enormous deviation from rectangularity of some of the sense-data, and therefore distinguish between "looks" and "looks$_{(ph)}$ ". Even more surprising are statements which Price makes about things bigger than a match-box. He speaks of looking edgewise at 'the square tower across the quad' and seeing two of its sides, and he says 'if I had been within the range of perfect stereoscopy, there would have been no distortion' (p. 219). But there is *no* place, near or far, from which two sides of such a tower both look$_{(ph)}$ rectangular. If Price's account of nuclear sense-data had received promptly the criticism it deserved, a generation of philosophers would not have been tempted to attribute to visual sense-data properties which fit them to form families which could deputize for the three-dimensional solids of common sense.

Philosophers who use "sense-datum" have defeated one of their purposes, namely to give theory-neutral descriptions of perceptual experience, through failing to distinguish the phenomenological from the other uses of verbs like "look" and "appear", and through giving priority to their other goal, i.e. getting incorrigible statements. Have they then succeeded in the latter aim? The answer must be NO. Their apparent success turns out to be a Pyrrhic victory. The supposedly hard facts expressed in sense-datum statements are soft and elastic. Such statements have commonly been equated with how things appear, meaning, indiscriminately, appear$_{(ph)}$ and/or appear *to be*. But even the philosophers who have recently recognized the need to say ' "looks", etc., in the phenomenological sense', have not recognized that sense-datum statements are still very elastic. The findings of Thouless described in chapter 1 reveal that when people are asked how things look in the phenomenological sense, their answers vary very widely. Looking at a tilted disc under exactly the same conditions, people matched its apparent$_{(ph)}$ shape with ellipses of very different proportions. And similarly wide variation was found in responses concerning apparent$_{(ph)}$ size and apparent$_{(ph)}$ whiteness. The only rules which would make sense-datum statements hard facts are rules which make them hard to verify. We should have to define "the properties of a sense-datum" in terms of the apparent$_{(ph)}$ properties of a perceived object, and equate "apparent$_{(ph)}$ shape" with what Thouless called 'perspectival shape', "apparent$_{(ph)}$ size" with what Price later called 'field of view size'; and then concede that seeing the shape or size that a thing *really* looks$_{(ph)}$ requires effort and practice, or else conditions which remove the clues which enable one to recognize the real shapes, sizes, and distances of the thing.

Getting indubitable statements is a Pyrrhic victory if it is achieved by the methods adopted by Ayer or Price—the adoption of arbitrary rules which imply that anything that a person says goes, when he says how things 'look', etc. The reason why Ayer and others have wanted incorrigible statements is to provide foundations for all empirical knowledge. This purpose is frustrated, if, in making these basic statements, whatever a person says goes. Austin made this point forcibly in a footnote in *Sense and Sensibilia*:

> to stipulate that a sense-datum just is whatever the speaker takes it to be —so that if he *says* something different it must be a different sense-datum—amounts to making non-mendacious sense-datum statements true by *fiat*; and if so, how could sense-data be, as they are also meant to be, non-linguistic entities *of* which we are aware, *to* which we refer, that against which the factual truth of all empirical statements is ultimately to be tested? (p. 113).

I have tried to show, as Austin did not, *how* commonly accepted rules for a sense-datum language amount to 'making non-mendacious statements true by *fiat*'. Austin's own account of our uses of "appears", "looks", etc., is, however, scarcely better than Ayer's, if one is looking for recognition of the difference between phenomenological and other uses of these verbs.[11]

Could Ayer meet the criticisms which we have levelled against his earlier writings? He might argue that his own use of "sense-datum" has been theory-neutral in that he has claimed that 'the sense-datum language' and 'the material-object language' are inter-translatable, are alternative ways of describing the very same facts. However the neutrality suggested in chapter 1 of *Foundations of Empirical Knowledge* was only apparent. For throughout this book, Ayer equates 'empirical facts' with *facts about sense-data* (as Austin pointed out in chapter IV of *Sense and Sensibilia*). And this view is retained in his later writings. In *The Problem of Knowledge* (1956), Ayer wrote that 'in referring as we do to physical objects we are elaborating *a theory* with respect to the evidence of our senses' (p. 147; my italics). And in 1967, in a paper[12] answering Austin's criticisms, Ayer revises his terminology but little else. He mentions that 'the sense-datum theorist' uses words like "look" and "appear" in 'the purely phenomenal sense' (p. 130), but does not recognize that this sense needs explanation, and scrutiny. He substitutes for "sense-datum statement" the term "experiential statement", and for "sense-datum" expressions like "visual pattern" or "visual presentation". The new terminology is introduced as being theory-neutral, by saying for example: 'If I may speak of a visual presentation in an entirely neutral sense, which carries no implication about the status of what is presented . . .' (p. 124). Yet Ayer jumps with astonishing speed to the conclusion that Realism is false. His only ostensible arguments for this conclusion are these: (i) that 'as I have construed expressions like 'directly see', it would be contradictory to speak of directly seeing material things, or any parts of them' (p. 128), (ii) 'that whereas statements which refer to physical objects are always in some sense proleptic, experiential statements are not' (p. 133).

It seems too charitable to call (i) an argument. It is simply a reminder of how Ayer has used "directly see" since 1940,[13] i.e. as a verb which *only* takes sense-datum terms as its grammatical objects. Indeed is (ii) an argument? It seems to be simply a repetition of the first clause in his definition of "experiential statement", while forgetting the second clause which implies that such a statement is theory-neutral. His definition is: 'a statement which does not go beyond the evidence, in the sense that that it carries no implication about the status of what is seen' (p. 119). For what Ayer means by "proleptic", when he says that physical object statements are, and experiential statements are not, proleptic, is simply this: that they involve prediction, or anticipation, of experiences which would be obtained by *further* observation. If I describe what I glance at as 'a tomato', I am indeed going beyond my evidence, beyond what is sense-given. My statement would be 'experiential', on Ayer's definition, if I confined the description of what I see to 'something red and shiny, round and bulgy'. But there is nothing in such a description which precludes this 'something' from *being* the front surface of a tomato as we Realists conceive it, i.e. as a solid which is 'all present and correct' at each moment of its history. Presumably Ayer's rejection of Realism in this paper was based not on the grounds he offered for it here, but on the traditional so-called 'argument from illusion'.

In some respects the positions which Ayer adopts in this 1967 paper are more extreme than in his earlier writings. The sensible-quality language which dispenses with all reference to physical things was said in 1956 to be 'not inconceivable', i.e. logically possible. The 1967 paper ends with the claim that *we* could construct such a language 'with sufficient ingenuity and labour', i.e. that it is possible in practice. Then what can we make of Ayer's claim in this paper that 'every *statement* which claims perception of a physical object is founded on an experiential *statement*' (p. 132; my italics). How could the statements which we do make about physical things be founded on statements in a language which does not exist, which *could* be constructed (or is 'not inconceivable')? If Ayer had said that all statements or beliefs about physical things are founded on sensory experiences, on the sensing of sense-data, this would have been intelligible, and a way of expressing a rule for using "sense-datum" which is adopted by all who use it. But Ayer presents his thesis as one concerning different kinds of *statements*. He does so because he wishes to represent his subject matter as being 'logic', and because he recognizes that logical relationships hold only between statements and not between the (other) things which we use words to talk about. Ayer does not explicitly refer to what is, I think, the most damaging of Austin's criticisms: that Ayer had been making non-mendacious statements about sense-data true by *fiat*. He does, however, amend the principle that sense-datum statements are incorrigible; but only to the extent of adopting 'the slightly weaker principle that the subject [the speaker] is the final authority with regard to their truth'. He adds: 'The criterion for saying that his description was mistaken will be his own decision to revise it' (p. 138). What did Ayer mean here by "the criterion"? Though "criterion" is one of the most popular jargon-words in recent philosophy, its users scarcely ever explain their usage. Sometimes they use "A is the criterion for saying B" to mean 'A provides a logically conclusive reason for saying B'. In that case Ayer's last-quoted sentence would mean that if a person offers successively several incompatible statements about how something looks$_{(ph)}$ or had looked$_{(ph)}$ to him, other people are logically obliged to accept his most recent report. Sometimes philosophers use "criterion" in a weaker sense (the *OED* sense) to mean simply: empirical evidence for judging. In that case Ayer's last-quoted sentence would mean, presumably, that *the* evidence (the only evidence?) that other people could have that something looks$_{(ph)}$ or had looked$_{(ph)}$ so and so to John is that this is what John has said most recently. Against either of these interpretations of Ayer's statement we may surely urge that, for example, the subjects in Thouless's experiment who matched the tilted disc with an almost circular ellipse may be told that they have simply failed to notice how the disc really looked$_{(ph)}$ to them from there. I should say this even if the subject had re-affirmed, refused to revise, his original description.

The reasons for my excursion into psychology in chapter 1 should now be clear. If a reader wishes a summary of the present rather complicated chapter, he should re-read its opening paragraph.

Part Three

# Can Realism be Reconciled with the Phenomenological Facts?

# 8
# Some Preliminary Adjudication

THERE are some gaps and weaknesses in my defence of Realism to which I must now draw attention. Notice first that my critique of 'the' sense-datum language does not show that it is impossible to design some such language which *is* theory-neutral. There are, of course, obvious dangers in using nouns like "sense-datum", "sensum" or "sense-impression", namely that such esoteric nouns be taken, as they have by nearly all who have used them, as names for things of an esoteric kind. Can we dispense with technical terms? Many contemporary philosophers have claimed that everything that can be said with the help of technical jargon can be said more simply in plain English; and have followed this policy, except when introducing new jargon to classify the functions of *words*. Warnock has proposed that we dispense with technical terms like "immediate perception". He says that he does not know of any 'familiar (intelligible) form of words' which meets our requirements except: "It seems to me now as if I were seeing [or hearing, etc.] . . ." (*Berkeley*, p. 168). However, the requirement which he here had in mind was simply avoiding the risk of error, the quest for incorrigible statements. Warnock's formula does achieve this purpose, but it seems to be unduly cautious, for "I think I see" or "I seem to see" would surely suffice. Each person is the final authority on what he *thinks* he sees, what he sees something *as*. Warnock's formula conveys more hesitation than "I think I see an M". Moreover, by using the subjunctive—"as if I *were* seeing an M", instead of "as if I *see* (*am seeing*) an M"—it suggests that the speaker thinks that it cannot really be an M which he is seeing. So his formula, if taken, as Warnock intends, as everyday English, seems apt only for reporting perceptual experiences which the speaker thinks or suspects to be an illusion or hallucination.

If Warnock's form of words were used for giving phenomenal descriptions, it would often be inappropriate. When something looks$_{(ph)}$ elliptical and brown, it would be misleading to convey this by saying 'It seems to me now as if I were seeing something elliptical and brown.' One can often be at least as confident about one's description of how something looks$_{(ph)}$ as one is in saying that one is seeing a round tilted penny. "Elliptical" and "brown" cover many distinct shapes and shades, so their use in describing how something looks$_{(ph)}$ leaves considerable lattitude. My chief objection to Warnock's formula is that it is usable for expressing, *very* tentatively, *both* phenomenal descriptions *and* estimates of the physical properties of perceived objects. In any critical discussion of perception, philosophical or scientific, it is essential not to confuse these different types of statement. If psychologists investigating perception fail to convey to their subjects which type of report they are soliciting, their findings are ambiguous; and the same goes for other scientists who investigate perception. The Optical Society of America has attempted to standardize a technical terminology to avoid confusion *inter alia* between estimates of the colour of a physical surface and what I have called 'sense-given colour' (what they call 'aperture colour').[1] Why should philosophers seek to ban philosophers from using technical terms? Any critical thinking about any subject requires that the thinker should remove the ambiguities with which everyday English abounds, should draw whatever distinctions are needed for his own purposes. In what follows, I shall, however, where possible, use "sense-given" and "looks"$_{(ph)}$, etc., in preference to the noun "sense-datum".

Let us review my earlier refutation of the argument from the phenomenal variability of the penny. That argument was shown to be invalid, and to be a by-product of confusing different uses of "real". To show this is *not*, however, to demonstrate the truth of Realism. Warnock wrote as if he thought that Realism can be justified simply by making emphatic statements like: 'To normal observers in ordinary daylight things *look* the colours they really *are* . . . sugar *is* sweet because it tastes so to normal people.'[2] To argue thus seems to involve the very confusion, between different uses of "real", which has generated the argument from phenomenal variability. 'To normal observers . . . things *look* the colours they really *are*' is, presumably, a reminder of the fact that we use "the real colour of so and so" to mean, roughly, 'the colour it looks$_{(ph)}$ to normal people in normal circumstances'. It is invalid to infer from this linguistic convention any conclusions about what is or is not real in the existential sense: *either* the conclusion that what exists in my visual field when the penny looks$_{(ph)}$ shiny-white is not the penny itself, *or* the conclusion, which Warnock seems to draw, that, when the penny looks round and brown, what exists in my visual field is the penny. When "its real colour (shape)" is contrasted with "its apparent colour (shape)", "real" is not being used in the existential sense. If we ask which colours or shapes are real in *this* sense, presumably we must say that all the colours and shapes that are visible are real. They are not unreal *qua* non-existent.

Admittedly Realism is presupposed by our everyday dictions, but so are many other questionable beliefs. For example, we speak of a person *having* a body and of his *having* a mind, as if *he* were something distinct from each. If English grammar is your map for learning about the natures of the things we talk about, you will need another map to help you interpret this one. Warnock's use of this map is not consistent. He says 'sugar *is* sweet because it tastes so to normal people'.[3] Then we would expect him to say 'fire *is* warm because it feels so to normal people'. But what he says is: 'The fire's quality of being pleasantly warm is . . . what the fire is said to have which does, or would, *occasion* pleasant feelings of warmth in normally sensitive people who do not get too close to it.' (My italics.) This at least strongly suggests that he is giving a causal account of the ascription of warmth to the fire, and not merely of the meaning of "pleasantly warm". In that case "the tomato *is* red" should be rendered 'the tomato's redness is what the tomato has which occasions red sense-data in normal people in daylight'. A case for Realism cannot rest upon reminders of our everyday distinction between 'real' and 'apparent' perceptible properties; since "real", in this sense, needs to be defined in terms of how things look$_{(ph)}$, taste$_{(ph)}$, etc. *to normal human observers*; and since it is a matter of convenience which properties we call 'real' and which 'apparent'. As Quinton has said,[4] we might, if we took to living in fluorescently-lit subterranean caves, choose to describe as their real colours the colours things look (i.e., presumably, look$_{(ph)}$) in this lighting.

In chapter 5, our convention for using "the real colour of" was defended on the ground that the conditions implicitly referred to, including normal daylight, are *optimal* conditions for discriminating colours. But this is questionable. Consider the fact described by Don Locke in these words: 'Stamp collectors use ultra-violet light to bring out slight differences in the colours of stamps.'[5] And Locke tells us that stamps which, in daylight, look exactly the same shade of *green,* look different shades of *violet* in ultra-violet light; yet he draws the conclusion that ultra-violet light shows that they are different shades of *green.* This was inconsistent, for Locke had just endorsed the convention that "the real colour of" means 'the colour seen by a normal percipient under standard conditions' (p. 99); which implies that the stamps are really of the same shade of green. Our convention, which Locke endorses, debars him from saying that ultra-violet light brings out (reveals) differences in the colours of things. Locke ought to have concluded either that ultra-violet light makes things look$_{(ph)}$ colours other than their real colours, or that we should revise our present convention for using "the real colour of". This we could do, and in future may do, since this convention was not designed to cope with a world in which different types of artificial lighting are common.

Readers may have noticed that, when defending Realism, I sometimes quoted arguments used by others. They may have guessed that this was because I could not conscientiously use them myself. The variation in the phenomenal colours of things due to states of the observer's body is a case in point. I cited arguments used by Price and Warnock which are short enough to sound plausible. Price suggests that all that the empirical evidence establishes is that some sense-data are dependent on the CNS in respect of *some* of their qualities; for example, that jaundice alters the colour of visual sense-data but not their so-called primary qualities. When Price used this argument he was, however, advocating Sensibilism, not defending Realism. If a Realist borrows Price's argument, he is exposed to a formidable objection. As Berkeley asked in his *First Dialogue*:

> How can you then conclude from sight, that figures exist without, when you acknowledge colours do not; the sensible appearance [i.e. the sense-datum] being the very same with regard to both? (p. 235.)

Or, as he put it earlier:

> doth it not follow, that where the one [a secondary quality, e.g. colour] exist, there necessarily the other [a primary quality, e.g. shape] exist likewise?' (p. 225.)

If, when you look at a tomato, the visible colour depends on your CNS and exists in you, how could the visible shape exist outside you and be the surface of the tomato?

Warnock's short way with the problem was to say 'if the conditions, or the observer's sense-organs, are abnormal, *of course* things will seem to be other than they really are. Of course a colour-blind man makes mistakes about colours.' Of course. "Colour-blind" *means* unable to discriminate some colours. And what else is meant here by speaking of sense-organs being 'abnormal'? Not *any* unusual state, for example, being at 96 or 101 degrees Fahrenheit, which does not usually make things look other than they are. Presumably "abnormal" here means: in a state in which things seem to be other than they really are! But two tautologies are scarcely sufficient to dispose of our present problem.

Let us now review the arguments which I used to supplement Stebbing's brusque justification of the physical reality of colours. Here I was using a pattern of argument which many recent philosophers have deemed decisive. Though I did not distinguish them earlier, two distinct arguments are involved:

(i) A ripe tomato is a paradigm case of a red object, and is also a paradigm case of a physical object. There are ripe tomatoes, so there are red physical objects. Q.E.D.

(ii) We communicate information by using "red". We could not have learned to use this word as we do, except by means of so-called ostensive definitions, that is, unless we had heard people uttering "red" on occasions when our attention was drawn to exemplars of things which are called 'red'. Such learning and teaching is possible only if the exemplars are publicly observable, and if the relevant property of such exemplars, e.g. the colour shared by ripe tomatoes, human blood, etc., is publicly observable. So the fact that we use "red" as we do implies that redness is a publicly observable property of publicly observable objects. Q.E.D.

It would have been reasonable to use the latter argument before colour-blindness had been discovered and investigated. But not now. To see how this argument had been undermined before it was invented, we must consider the relevant facts.[6] It is not safe to rely on our intuitive understanding of terms introduced by scientists without finding what they use them to talk about. About 3 people in 100,000 (called 'monochromats') cannot distinguish any except the so-called neutral colours (greys, black and white)—they match the 'colours' they see in daylight with those that they see in twilight, when only their rods can function. Between 2 and 3 per cent of white males have only two of the three types of cones involved in normal human colour vision. They are called 'dichromats'. They can be made to see all the colours which they can distinguish by different mixtures of light of *two* wavelengths, almost always a short and a medium wavelength. Such people are completely unable to discriminate colours in the green-yellow-red region of the visible spectrum. A single specific wavelength which makes others see blue-green makes them see white or grey, because it stimulates equally their two types of cone. About 6 per cent of white males have three types of cone but one of these is abnormally insensitive. They are called 'anomalous trichromats'. They have poor discrimination in the green-yellow-red range. Whether it is the 'red-responsive' or the 'green-responsive' cones which are insensitive in a particular case can be determined by finding in what proportions long and medium wavelengths have to be mixed to make the person see yellow. Notice that this type of defect is a matter of degree. The percentage of people classified as anomalous trichromats depends on how large a deviation from the *average* person's colour discrimination one decides to count as abnormal. The current convention is to classify about 90 per cent of males as having normal colour vision, but the convention could be so to classify 50 per cent, or even 10 per cent. It is commonly assumed that, for the 90 per cent of males normally classified as having normal colour vision, the same light-stimuli make them see the same colours. This assumption cannot be justified. Ralph M. Evans sums up the position thus:

> individuals vary tremendously in matching colours . . . the average can almost be described as never occurring in practice . . . A rough estimate indicates that a perfect match by a perfect 'average' observer would probably be unsatisfactory for something like 90 per cent of all observers because variations between observers is very much greater than the smallest colour differences which they can distinguish.[7]

Though Evans does not say so, for he was writing before the three-cone theory of colour vision had been confirmed, presumably the variations between observers are due to differences in the relative sensitivity of their three types of cones. The point to be stressed is this. If people are given the task of matching colours, i.e. of reporting whether or not two light-stimuli look exactly similar in colour, nearly all pairs of people will disagree in some cases, some pairs in many cases, one of them saying 'distinctly different' when the other says 'indistinguishable'.

Consider the situation where another person reports that two surfaces or lights look indistinguishable in colour to him, yet to you, viewing them in exactly the same conditions, they look decidedly different in colour. In such a case you *know* that the shade which the other person sees cannot be the same as *both* of the different shades that you see. And you have no grounds for assuming that the shade he sees is the same as *either* of those that you see. If the other person cannot distinguish things which you see as red and green, then for all you can tell he sees each as some shade which you would call 'red', or would call 'green', or 'yellow', or 'brown', etc. And though only about 2 per cent of males cannot distinguish reds and greens, most of us cannot distinguish many pairs of samples which many others can discriminate. These facts undermine the common-sense assumption that 'we', or nearly all of us, see the same colours whenever our eyes are stimulated in the same ways, the assumption that people who agree in calling grass 'green' and tomatoes 'red' must be seeing the same colours when they look at such things. Agreement in the application of colour-names to everyday objects concealed the existence of colour-blindness for almost the whole of human history; until 1794, when John Dalton was led to publish an account of his own colour vision, whose defectiveness he had recognized because he could not distinguish chemical substances which looked the same in colour to him, but not to his laboratory assistants. Colour-blindness was unnoticed and unnamed for so long because colour-blind people usually agree with others in applying colour-names to everyday objects. Occasionally they make statements from which their defect can be inferred; for example, surfaces which are red, dark yellow, and green may all be described by them as 'brown'. But dichromats who suffer from complete red-green colour blindness have, like the rest of us, been taught to apply "green" to grass and summer foliage and "red" to ripe tomatoes and human blood. They can, of course, nearly always discriminate a red object on a green background, and vice versa. The petals of a poppy differ visibly from the grass in so many other respects apart from hue, e.g. in brightness, shininess and visible texture, and in distance when within the range of stereoscopic vision. Diagnosis of colour-blindness requires removal of all other visible differences except hue.

It turns out then that the argument for Realism regarding colours which we are considering is broken-backed. The facts that we all use words like "red" and nearly always agree in their everyday applications do not establish that what we are applying them to are *publicly observable* qualities. Each of us has learnt to associate "red" with the shades which *he himself* sees when he looks at ripe tomatoes, British pillar boxes, etc. A person not familiar with the findings of colorimetry takes it for granted that the colour *he* sees when he looks at a tomato is the same colour seen in it by other people, or at least by people not colour-blind (a qualification which became incorporated in common sense only during the nineteenth century). But this assumption is no longer tenable. Indeed two people, A and B, might have colour vision which, on all obtainable evidence, *is* normal and perfect, in that they never disagree with each other in colour matching and never fail to distinguish samples which others distinguish. Yet in B the mechanism for colour perception might have been reversed by a genetic mutation, so that stimulation of B's cones which are most sensitive to long wavelengths might cause in him the kind of brain-processes which, in A, are caused by stimulation of the cones most sensitive to short wavelengths, and vice versa. Then, although A and B agree in calling tomatoes 'red' and a clear sky 'blue', the sense-given shades which one calls 'reds' would be shades which the other calls 'blues' and vice versa. If this possibility is fulfilled, as it may be, it would be impossible to verify this on the evidence of the testimony and behaviour of A and B. Confronted with this argument, a philosopher might appeal to the verification principle and say: since we cannot verify that two people who agree in naming the colours of public objects apply the same names to the same shades, it is *meaningless* to suppose that, or to ask whether, they do. But a Realist is not free to argue thus if he has used the popular argument for Realism which we are now considering: that the fact that we have learned to use colour-words implies that *the same colour is seen* by those who give and by those who receive ostensive definitions. In any case, the verification principle is clearly being abused in the counter-argument. 'A and B are seeing the same colour' must be meaningful if 'A and B are *not* seeing the same colour' is meaningful; and statements of the latter form are meaningful, and they can often be verified. We have conclusive empirical evidence for saying, in many cases, that A is *not* seeing at least one of two shades which B is seeing, namely when A reports, and his behaviour confirms, that the colours of two objects are indistinguishable for him, and B says, and shows, that he can discriminate their colours.

Let us turn to the Paradigm Case argument. A ripe tomato is a paradigm case both of a red thing and of a physical object, it is the sort of thing by reference to which we have given "red" and "physical object" the meanings which they have; so it would be flagrantly inconsistent to deny *either* that it is red *or* that it is a physical object. But the facts concerning colour vision which we have just described prevent this argument from establishing what the Realist wants it to, namely that colours are *publicly observable* qualities of things. It establishes only that *for each person* it would be inconsistent to deny that the colour that *he* sees when *he* looks at a ripe tomato in daylight is a shade which *he* calls 'red'. The Paradigm Case argument may be deployed differently: for example, by reminding us that we do have experiences which are correctly described as 'seeing a tomato', etc., and that seeing a tomato is a paradigm case of *seeing* (directly) a physical object. But what follows? This gambit does refute the Representative theory if this is presented as denying the truth of 'We see physical objects.' It does not, however, refute Phenomenalism or Sensibilism which do not deny the truth of such statements, nor of the Representative theory *if* it were presented as an analysis of what we mean by such statements. When the use of an expression presupposes beliefs about the things to which it is applied, we cannot justify these beliefs merely by issuing reminders that the expression *is* used. When an Archbishop shuts his eyes and starts 'O God please . . .', this is a paradigm case of addressing God, is the sort of thing by reference to which "addressing God" is given the meaning that it has. Does the fact that this phrase is used establish, as D. Z. Phillips has argued,[8] not only that people who pray know how to use "God", but also that they 'know God'? Surely not. Expressions like "addressing God" and "physical object" have a connotation as well as a denotation.

"Denotation" means the set of *things to which* a term is applied. "Connotation" means, roughly, the *properties* which we ascribe to things in applying the term. "Addressing God", as this phrase is normally understood by Christians, presupposes the existence of a personal God who hears and sometimes heeds prayers. The use of "physical object" by Realists presupposes, e.g., that the things to which it is applicable continue to exist when not being perceived by anyone, and that they then still possess properties of kinds perceptible by us. These articles of faith cannot be proved merely by reminding us that "physical object" has a denotation, any more than the existence of a personal God can be proved by reminders that "addressing God" has a denotation.

Stebbing used the Paradigm Case argument against Eddington when she reminded us that planks are standard examples of solid objects. But what does "solid" *connote* when it is applied to planks, tables, etc. To say 'M is solid' involves attributing to M the properties of being continuously filled by matter and of not being penetrable without having some of this matter displaced. But if, as physicists claim, a particle can pass through a plank without displacing any part or component thereof, then planks do not, after all, have all the properties which had hitherto been connoted by "solid". Then we are not entitled to dismiss what Eddington was saying on the ground that he had invented a new sense of "solid" unrelated to the old sense. This may be one of the cases where our common sense beliefs have to be revised, and not merely reaffirmed with the help of italics. Fortunately the required amendment to Realism is no more damaging than that which is involved in conceding that we see very remote objects where, and as, they were at an earlier time. "Solid", in the relevant sense, can be amended to mean: impenetrable *except* by so-called fundamental particles.

The most vulnerable feature of my defence of Realism was, I think, in making explicit something presupposed by our commonsense conception of perception, without making explicit the implications. Our everyday uses of verbs like "see" presuppose that the function of the physiological processes on which perception depends is selective, that is, it reveals, discloses, *some* physical things and *some* of their properties. I glossed over the main problem which then arises, namely, how then can we stop short of the paradoxical conclusion that each of the physical things that we can perceive *has* all the properties which it ever appears$_{(ph)}$ to have. It would be arbitrary in the extreme to maintain that processes in the CNS reveal qualities inherent in physical things, but only when the conditions comply with the rather vague and arbitrary conventions implicit in our uses of "real property of"; to maintain, for example, that the CNS reveals the shape of the penny, but only when it is viewed from in front, and reveals the colour of the penny but only when diffuse daylight, or its equivalent, is suitably reflected by it; and to maintain that what we see under other conditions are, after all, sense-data generated by processes in the CNS. This position would be incoherent; for when the penny looks$_{(ph)}$ round, it may look$_{(ph)}$ black or shiny-white, and when it looks$_{(ph)}$ brown it commonly looks$_{(ph)}$ elliptical. The view which we are considering is not the same as Sensibilism, according to which each physical thing is a family of sensibilia, each of the latter being a distinct entity. A Realist will insist that a physical object is a single three-dimensional solid. Then what have to be multiplied, according to the selective theory, are the inherent properties of such an object.

Is it nonsense to say that a penny *has* all of the shapes it looks$_{(ph)}$? I suggest we can make sense of saying this. The penny looks$_{(ph)}$ different shapes and sizes from different places; for example, round and two angular degrees in diameter *from here*, elliptical and five degrees in width and two in height, *from there*. It projects different shapes and sizes at different places, whether or not these places are occupied by observers. It sounds a bit Irish to say that it is an *inherent* property of the penny that it is round-from-here; for 'from-here' indicates that the property in question is a relational property. "An inherent property of M" would normally be used to refer to a property whose description does not involve mentioning M's relationships to anything else. But whatever name we use to refer to the properties which we are considering, these properties are *public*; they are specified by reference only to places in our common space of three-dimensional solids. The phenomena referred to as 'perspectival distortion' provide no grounds for concluding that what each of us sees are private entities generated by his own CNS.

But what about colours? This is where the shoe pinches. Just how hard it pinches will become clear in the next chapter. Hitherto philosophers seem to have noticed that the colours we see are altered by the states of our bodies only in cases like that of severe jaundice. Had that been so there would be no new problem. Jaundice makes things $\text{look}_{(ph)}$ yellow because bile gets into the eyes, so it is equivalent to wearing yellow spectacles. What creates a different problem is the fact that, and the extent to which, the phenomenal colours of a thing may vary, when it is viewed from the same place, owing to changes in the CNS. In view of this, Realism regarding colours involves an extreme paradox. I have argued that there is no inconsistency in saying that a physical object, at a certain place, has many different shapes and sizes *from* various other places. It is, however, repugnant to common sense to conclude that each of the many different colours that a physical surface may $\text{look}_{(ph)}$ from the same place is an inherent quality of that surface. Yet the Selective theory implies this, by claiming that processes in the perceiver's CNS *reveal* properties which things have independently of their being perceived. If we apply this to colours, we shall have to conclude that the same surface of a physical object simultaneously possesses all the colours it can $\text{look}_{(ph)}$ from each of the places from which it is visible; and that in order to see many of its colours, we have to get our eyes or brains into unusual states.

To sum up. Many of the arguments which I presented in Part Two in defence of Realism are wholly inadequate for this purpose. The arguments purporting to show that colours are qualities inherent in physical things are conspicuously weak. The counter-arguments which I have used in the present chapter seem to show that Realism is untenable, at any rate so far as vision is concerned. The case for drawing this conclusion may be summarized thus. The processes in the sense-organs and the CNS on which perception depends must, presumably, function in one or other of two ways—revealing what is there or creating sense-data which represent what is there. If their function is to reveal what is there, we shall have to conclude that each physical surface simultaneously possesses many very different colours. The statement that the same surface cannot simultaneously be wholly and uniformly pervaded by different colours will be, not a truism, but the very opposite of the truth. The paradox disappears if what are visibly coloured are sense-data created by the CNS. The case for adopting this conclusion is very much stronger than was conveyed in chapter 3. I shall now support it by amplifying conclusions drawn from the science of colour vision which were presented too baldly in chapter 3.

# 9

# Some Facts about Colour Vision and their Theoretical Implications

---

WHAT is written about colour is often clouded by failure to make it clear:

(*a*) when reference is being made to colours, i.e. visible colour-qualities, and when to light as physicists conceive it, radiant energy, what Newton called 'red- (blue-, etc.) making Rays';

(*b*) when "M's colour" or "the colour M looks" is used to refer to the estimated or recognized normal-daylight colour of M, and when to M's phenomenal colour. (The phenomenal colour of M may e.g. be dull grey, or light green, when M is recognized as white paper in shadow.)

I have tried, but may sometimes have failed, to avoid these sources of obscurity.

In his book on Berkeley, Warnock wrote: 'Inspection of the terms and concepts of science might show us that the conclusions of scientists have in fact no tendency to *contradict* our ordinary judgements of perception' (p. 233). This hope might have been fulfilled, but it has not. To recognize this, there is, however, no short-cut which spares us the trouble of considering some of the facts which need to be explained and the explanations which scientists offer. The 'conceptual schemes' whereby physicists and physiologists explain colour vision were adumbrated in chapter 3. I pointed out that it is unintelligible to ascribe colour-qualities to light as it is conceived by physicists; and that there is no single physical feature shared by all the things in which the same colour 'visibly inheres'; and that it is not the case that there is a one–one correlation between the colours we see and the wavelengths of the lights which make us see them, that the relations are one–many, i.e. that for each colour there are very many mixtures of wavelengths which can make us see it.* I argued, however, in chapter 3 as if the colour that a person sees in a given direction is determined by the wavelengths in the light coming from that direction. That assumption is false. The facts which show this are, however, complex, and I shall lead up to them by stages. The earlier part of the chapter will also serve another purpose—to indicate why scientific theories deserve our credence.

First, however, I must explain how I am using "colours" and "a colour". Philosophers have often used colour-names as if they were colour-blind, saying things like: red(ness) is, or "red" names, a simple quality. According to G. E. Moore, "yellow" and "good" are alike in that each denotes 'one simple unique object of thought'.[1] Moore's claim about "good" has been a popular target for criticism, but his claim about "yellow" has passed unchallenged. Experimental evidence shows that there are about ten million colours distinguishable by people of normal vision.[2] Anyone can verify that this number is *very* large. Take a child's paintbox containing, say, 30 pigments. For *each* of these you can produce a series of slightly different colours by mixing it in different proportions with *each* of 29 others. The English language provides only about 30 words which are used solely or primarily as colour-names and only a few hundred if we include words whose use as colour-names is derived from the colours of the stuff or the things that they denote, e.g. "cobalt", "lilac", or "olive". Philosophers sometimes distinguish 'determinable' and 'determinate' properties. For example, being coloured is a determinable, being warm-coloured a sub-determinable, and being red, it is said, a determinate quality. But this will not do, even if what we are classifying are English words. "Red" is a sub-determinable, with terms like "scarlet", "crimson", and "brick-red" coming below it. But if what we are classifying are, not words, but colours, no colour-word names a determinate colour since each is applicable to many distinguishable shades. (Including "white". Soap salesmen have encouraged us to use "whiter" and "whitest".)

* Philosophers who invoke the science of colour vision usually assume a one–one correlation between colours and wavelengths. Two exceptions are J. J. C. Smart, e.g. in 'Colours', *Philosophy*, 1961, and K. Cambell in 'Colour' in *Contemporary Philosophy in Australia*, 1969, ed. R. Brown and C. D. Rollins.

I use "colours" in such a way that two colours are different if they are distinguishable in hue *or* saturation *or* brightness. I avoid the terms "hue" and "saturation" wherever possible, because they are used in colorimetry as technical terms, and "hue" does not then mean what it means in everyday English. The three 'dimensions' in which scientists find it useful to order millions of colours are adapted to fit facts and theories about colour mixture. Scientists distinguish some conveniently small number of 'hues', e.g. seven (Newton), ten (Munsell), sixteen (Helson) or twenty (the Committee on Colorimetry of the Optical Society of America). They treat all colours as variations on these few themes. When one looks for the first time at the samples which they bracket together as being 'of the same hue', one gasps; one wants to protest that, for example, the colours which they include in the family of a certain shade of yellow include colours which *we* call off-whites and greys, khakis, olives, duns, and dark browns.[3] It is perilous to use technical terms like "hue" and "saturation" if your audience (or you) are unaware of the differences between their technical and their everyday uses.

In Part One, I divided the arguments against Realism into two classes—Phenomenological and Science-inspired. This is a rather arbitrary division. Scientific studies of perception have started from phenomenological facts, e.g. those which Newton recorded when describing what he saw when he passed light through prisms. What scientists set out to explain are facts concerning how things look and/or look$_{(ph)}$. There are hosts of such facts which are incoherent and baffling if we adopt a Realist theory concerning colours, but which become connected, intelligible, and predictable once we understand the scientists' explanations. I shall start by citing a few such facts. A reader can easily verify some of them, and regarding those which he cannot, he can confirm that they have been verified by careful experiments:

(1) Gold-leaf which is reflecting normal day-light normally looks yellow, but when it lines the inside of a suitably curved cup or bowl it looks quite a deep red, and when it is held between the eye and the sun or a lamp it may look blue-green.

(2) If you look at port wine in a slim conical glass held against the light, its colours range from pale yellow at the bottom, through orange, to ruby-red, and, as the reader can verify for himself, a bathful would look almost black.

(3) A mixture of blue paint and yellow paint looks some shade of green. (Usually—but the *colours* of pigments do not enable us to make reliable predictions about the colour of their mixture.) Experience in mixing paints would not lead one to expect that mixing blue and yellow light would ever produce white light. But the laws concerning colours yielded by mixing lights are very different from those concerning the results of mixing pigments. Visibly white light can be produced by mixing two lights which, separately, look indigo-blue and yellow, and also by mixing lights which look red and cyan (blue-green), and by mixing lights of many other pairs of spectral colours.

(4) If one illuminates things in a synthetic white light which contains only two specific wavelengths, some things look and look$_{(ph)}$ their familiar daylight colours and some look$_{(ph)}$ and often look dramatically different. Using light composed of lights which separately looked yellow and blue, I have seen white paper looking$_{(ph)}$ white,* blue paper looking$_{(ph)}$ blue, and yellow paper looking$_{(ph)}$ yellow; but green paper looked$_{(ph)}$ dark blue and refused to look green, and a tomato looked$_{(ph)}$ a yellowish brown and refused to look red.

In *Berkeley* Warnock wrote: 'If the conditions are abnormal *of course* things will seem to be other than they really are... obviously an unusual light will alter the looks of things. Such cases are... not in the least disconcerting' (pp. 147–8). I found the phenomena just described disconcerting, since some things did, and some did not, look$_{(ph)}$ or look their daylight colours; and since knowledge of their daylight colours is useless by itself for predicting what colours things will look in unusual lighting. Would you not expect that in red light, things red in daylight would look redder than things having other daylight colours? But paper which is light *green* in daylight looks$_{(ph)}$ and looks redder than paper which in daylight is dull red.

Surely such facts cry out for explanation, as do the striking differences between the results of mixing coloured lights and of mixing coloured pigments. To reaffirm Realism regarding colours would be to preclude any attempt to explain the facts in question. The striking variations in the colours seen in gold-leaf and port

* Strictly it was off-white, or, in Newton's phrase, 'a faint anonymous colour'. The two wavelengths in the illuminant were not quite opposites in the Newtonian colour circle.

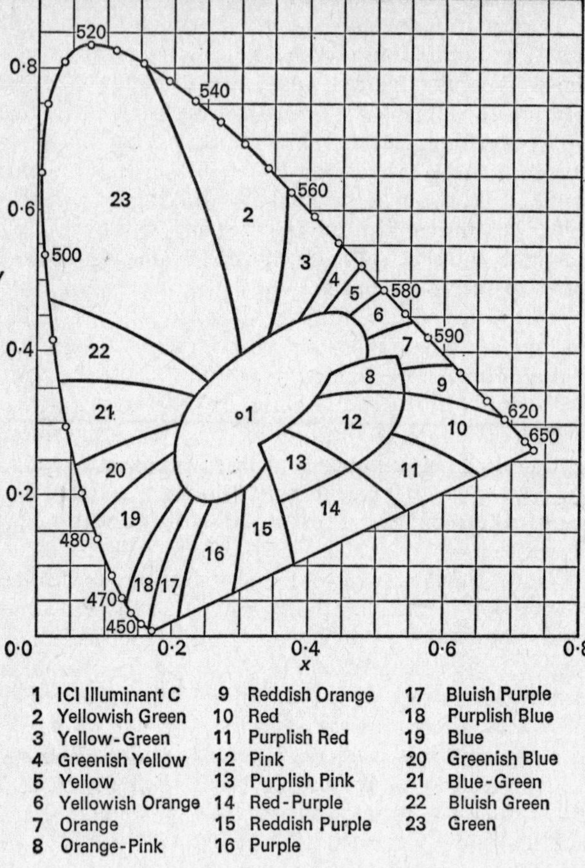


*Figure 4. The colour-triangle*

This is no longer triangular like its ancestor, introduced by J. C. Maxwell. Wavelengths are plotted round the circumference excluding the straight base-line, from the shortest wavelength (400 m$\mu$) at the left end of the base-line to the longest (700 m$\mu$) at the right end. The above diagram also gives a rough indication of the hues corresponding to different regions within the triangle. The inclusion of "ICI Illuminant C" in the list of colour-names is scarcely appropriate. The relevant colour-words would be "white or whitish". "ICI Illuminant C" refers to a light which is a 'satisfactory substitute for average daylight', and which is slightly wine cannot be *explained* by saying that their day-light colours 'inhere in' them, since all the different colours mentioned in paragraphs (3) and (4) *are* daylight colours. We say that the 'real' colour of port is ruby-red—because we usually view it in receptacles which make it look so. One could scarcely claim, however, that the other colours that port wine looks are 'variations on a common theme'. The perspectival distortions of a square (or a round) surface may be said to be 'variations on a common theme', a family of four-sided figures (or of ellipses). But yellow, orange, and black are very different from ruby-red, not variations on *that* theme. Nor are red and blue-green variations of golden-yellow.

The anomalous facts cited above become intelligible in the light of scientific theories. Let us start with the principles involved in mixing *lights* of different visible colours. As stated in chapter 3, normal human colour vision depends on our having three types of cones, which respond selectively to wavelengths in different regions of the spectrum. We see neutral colours (white, grey, or black, depending on the *strength* of the light) when the relative intensity of stimulation of the three types of cone is of a certain ratio, $x : y : z$. When the relative intensity of stimulation of the three types of cone has any ratio substantially different from this, we see other ('chromatic') colours. For any of the colours which a person can see, there are very many *different* mixtures of two or more specific wavelengths which can make him see that colour, because each of them stimulates his three types of cones in the *same* proportions. Pictorial devices have been invented which enable one to predict the shade seen when an 'average' human eye is stimulated by any given mixture of light of different wavelengths. Newton's colour circle was the first such device. For the last century a triangle has usually been used (see Figure 4). Such a diagram is a convenient way of presenting a great deal of information—experimentally

---

different in composition from one containing equal amounts of all the wavelengths in the visible spectrum. This diagram and the list of colour names is reproduced from Ralph M. Evans, *An Introduction to Color* (p. 232), with the kind permission of John Wiley & Sons, Inc. For an explanation of the colour-triangle and its uses in colorimetry, see Ralph M. Evans, op. cit., ch. XV, and Committee on Colorimetry, *The Science of Color*, ch. 7.

determined laws concerning the colours seen by an average observer when his eyes are stimulated by any possible mixture of lights of different wavelengths. On the circumference are plotted the wavelengths corresponding to the various spectral colours, and a point in the middle represents white light. The spacing is so arranged that any pair of wavelengths which are opposite, on a line through the centre, will, when mixed in certain proportions, produce light which is visibly white. And we can, from the triangle, read off the hue and saturation for any mixture of two or more wavelengths. Newton's prediction that 'All the Colours of the Universe' can be produced by 'compounding' lights which make us see pure spectral colours has proved to be correct. And we can be made to see most of the colours that we can distinguish by different mixtures of three wavelengths; and it does not matter which wavelengths are selected for this purpose, so long as one is from the short (B) waveband, one from the medium (G), and one from the long (R). But the laws represented by the colour-triangle apply only to mixtures of *light*. This kind of colour-mixing is called additive to contrast it with the mixing of coloured pigments. This is called 'subtractive' because each pigment (or any physical object) absorbs, subtracts, the wavelengths which it does not reflect. If a tomato reflects 70 per cent of the long and 10 per cent of the short wavelengths, is subtracts 30 per cent of the former and 90 per cent of the latter.

We are now in a position to explain the anomalous facts mentioned earlier. Why does a mixture of blue and yellow paints look green? This is because blue paint subtracts most of the long (R) wavelengths and much of the medium (G), and the yellow paint subtracts most of the short (B) wavelengths, and much of the medium; so the mixture subtracts most of the long and most of the short wavelengths and reflects, predominantly, the 'green-making rays'. On the other hand, an additive mixture of certain blue and yellow lights stimulates the three types of cones in the proportions which make us see white; and so it makes white paper reflecting it look white. Such light makes blue and yellow objects look their daylight colours because it contains 'blue-making' and 'yellow-making rays' for them to reflect. It makes the tomato look a yellowish brown because there are no 'red-making rays' for it to reflect, but it does reflect a little of the 'yellow-making rays', which at low intensities make us see browns.

Now consider the colours of port wine. Newton explained the facts thus:

Such a Liquor stops the indigo-making . . . Rays most easily, the blue-making Rays more difficultly, the green-making Rays still more difficultly and the red-making most difficultly . . . If the thickness of the Liquor be only so much as suffices to stop a competent number of the . . . indigo-making Rays, without diminishing much of the number of the rest, the rest must [by his laws for additive mixtures] compound to a pale yellow. But if the Liquor be so much thicker as to stop also a great number of blue-making Rays, and some of the green-making, the rest must compound [to] an orange.

And so on. A principle which is involved here is that if one centimetre of port transmits, say, 50 per cent of a certain wavelength, two centimetres will transmit (50 per cent × 50 per cent) = 25 per cent thereof. A similar principle explains why gold, lining a bowl, may look red. Gold reflects roughly a quarter of the green-making, half of the yellow-making, and three-quarters of the red-making rays; and these compound to yield a warm yellow. But most of the light emerging from the bowl has been reflected by *several* surfaces; and this changes the proportions of the different wavelengths. For example, light thrice reflected would have components in the following proportions of the incident light: 1/64 of the green-making, 1/8 of the yellow-making and 2/5 of the red-making.* Then the red-making rays are predominant. Gold-leaf, if it is thin enough, looks blue-green when held between the eye and the sun, because some of the light of the shorter wavelengths then passes through it. Such details may seem out of place in a philosophical essay. But unless one has sought and understood the sort of explanations which science provides of otherwise baffling facts, one is unlikely to recognize why scientific theories have such a strong claim on our credence.

The anomalous facts discussed so far are capable of being explained within the theoretical framework provided by Newton and still used by physicists; i.e. according to the principle that the colour you see in any direction is determined by the mixture of wavelengths reaching your eyes from *that* direction. We must now describe anomalous facts which are incompatible with this classical assumption. But let us start with some facts which, though they

* $(1/4)^3 = 1/64$, and so on.

require us to qualify the classical assumption, are too familiar to be called anomalous.

(1) *Colour-constancy and lightness-constancy.* The facts so referred to are that, for a wide variety of types of illumination, familiar objects are recognized as things which have certain daylight colours and degrees of lightness. In my terminology, they look the same in colour and lightness despite wide differences in how they look$_{(ph)}$. Helmholtz tried to reconcile such facts with the classical assumption by supposing that the latter applies to what I call 'the sense-given colours' in each part of one's visual field, and that 'we are accustomed and trained to form a judgement of the colours of bodies by eliminating the brightness . . . [and] the colour of the illumination'. These 'acts of judgement', he said, 'are always executed unconsciously and involuntarily'.[4] He provoked needless criticism by using the word "judgement". The facts may be described by saying that we automatically discount, make allowances for, the nature of the illumination, when we can recognize this and familiar objects which are illuminated by it. The ability to do this is obviously dependent on past experience. The kind of compensation which Helmholtz was discussing is not possible if one cannot recognize what it is that one is looking at or the nature of the light.

(2) *Simultaneous colour contrast.* This phrase refers to the familiar fact that things look$_{(ph)}$, and often look, differently coloured against different backgrounds. If you cut a piece of cyan paper into 3 squares, and place these on black, white, and yellow backgrounds, each looks (as well as looks$_{(ph)}$) very different in colour —green on the black ground, blue on the yellow, and much darker on the white than on the other two grounds. In laboratory conditions much more dramatic changes can be induced by contrast. In white light, and simply by increasing the brightness of the white background, an object changes from looking bright red to looking dull brown, or from looking white to looking black.[5] And in red illumination, subjects who did not know its daylight colour consistently described a piece of paper as looking greenish blue when it was on a white ground, as yellow when on a grey ground, and as bluish red when on a black ground. The daylight colour of the paper was purple![6] Notice that such facts render incredible Realism regarding colours. If a thing's visible colour inhered *in it*, how could this be changed so dramatically simply by changes in

what lies *behind* it? Do the phenomena of colour-contrast require only a qualification of the classical assumption described above? Many scientists try to get away with such a qualification, namely by saying that the colour seen in a certain direction is determined by the mixture of wavelengths coming from that direction, but that "the colour seen" is to mean here the aperture colour, and that "the aperture colour" is to mean the colour you *would* see *if* you looked through an aperture in a screen which cuts out any contrasting surrounding colours. But this will not do, since the aperture colour will vary according to the apparent colour of the *screen*. If such a screen is lit with strong red light, a weaker red light seen through the peephole may look grey or blue-green.[7] The classical assumption is valid only for 'aperture colours' arbitrarily defined as meaning e.g. the colour seen through a peephole in a *black* screen. It is convenient in colorimetry to adopt this arbitrary definition, but it would be wholly unjustifiable for *us* to say that the real colour of a tomato is the colour it looks$_{(ph)}$ when it is seen surrounded by black. And it would be preposterous to say that the colour the tomato now looks$_{(ph)}$ to me is the *different* colour that it *would* look$_{(ph)}$ *if* I saw it surrounded by black instead of by the colour by which it is now visibly surrounded! This draws attention to an asymmetry between the phenomenal colours of things and their phenomenal shapes and sizes. We can define "the shape" and "the size that M looks$_{(ph)}$ from a place P" so that, given the relative positions of M and P, this shape and size are determinate, are what I have been calling 'the perspectival shape' and 'the field of view size'. It would, however, be intolerably arbitrary to define "the colour M looks$_{(ph)}$ from P" in a way which implies that, given the relative positions of M and P and the nature of the lighting, there is only *one* determinate colour which M can look$_{(ph)}$ from P.

(3) *Successive colour contrasts.* If you fixate for 15 to 20 seconds on the spot in the middle of the green rectangle on the cover of this book and then look at the grey paper below, you will see on the latter three rectangles of different colours—pink in the middle, yellow on the left, and blue-green on the right. At least you will if your colour vision is normal and you wait for a few seconds. And if you look at some milk after gazing at a bright red bucket, the milk will look$_{(ph)}$ blue-green. So the classical assumption requires further revision. The colour that you see in a given direction D depends not only on the wavelengths in the light coming from that

direction, it depends also on the wavelengths to which the relevant parts of your retinas are currently adapted, *and*, as we saw in the last paragraph, it depends on the wavelengths coming from directions surrounding D. It is already clear that the classical assumption is false. It is inconsistent to go on treating it as true, while adding, as qualifications of it, clauses which in fact negate its content. Consider now an explanation of successive colour contrast which is given in textbooks:

> 'if the eye is exposed to green light, the green receptors, and to a much lesser extent the red and the blue receptors, are depressed in sensitivity . . . the higher the intensity and the longer the exposure, the slower is the recovery of sensitivity . . . While the depression lasts, the eye is deficient in response from the green receptor. It will see a low intensity non-selective stimulus as pink . . .'[8]

This explanation assumes that, in the green-adapted eye, the red- and blue-sensitive cones are responding *to what is there*, i.e. to the long and the short wavelengths reflected by the grey paper, while the medium wavelengths which are also being reflected by the paper evoke little or no response from the tired green receptors. But this is gratuitous; for if, after fixating on the green rectangle on the book-cover, you shut your eyes (or turn the lights out in a darkened room), the rectangles of colours complementary to those you had been seeing are still visible; and indeed their colours are then, for some people, more vivid. In this case it is clear that the colours that you see are created by your CNS.* Yet they can be 'projected' on to an external surface. The images seem bigger when you look at a more distant wall.

We must now consider the results of experiments conducted by Edwin G. Land[9] which decisively dispose of the classical assumption that the colour seen in any direction is determined by the wavelengths in the light coming from that direction. Land's technique involved taking two identical *black and white* photographs of the same scene, one through a filter which passed only light in the long-wave third of the visible spectrum, the other through a filter which passed only light in the middle third. Let us call the black and white positive photographs so produced the

* When I speak of colours being created 'by the CNS', I am including in the CNS the retina, 'a specialized part of the surface of the brain which has budded out', as Gregory puts it (*Eye and Brain*, p. 46).

long(wave) and the medium(wave) records. Land put these records into two projectors, and projected them on a screen 'in register', i.e. so that the two images were exactly superimposed. When the light used to project the long record was of a longer wavelength than that used to project the medium record, the picture seen on the screen contained shades of most of the colours for which we have names. And this happened *even when the light used in both projectors was yellow* and of wavelengths only slightly different (different by 1/20 of the range of the visible spectrum). This was an astonishing result. According to the laws of light mixture, two slightly different yellows combine to yield an intermediate shade of yellow. Yet here, when no wavelengths outside the 'yellow-making' range were available to stimulate their eyes, people saw pictures containing blues, greens, oranges, and reds, as well as blacks, whites, and greys. Moreover, when Land used light of the *longer* wavelength to project the *medium* record and vice versa, the colours seen in the resulting pictures were reversed, e.g. bluebells looked red and tomatoes looked blue.

In one of his experiments, Land used yellow sodium light (wavelength $589_{m\mu}$) alternatively to project the long record and to project the medium record. (In the former case, green light was used to project the medium record; in the latter, red light was used to project the long record.) In the latter case, the sodium light was the shortest wavelength stimulating their eyes, yet it enabled people to see blues and greens. In the former case, the sodium light was the longest wavelength present, yet it enabled people to see oranges and reds. The significance of such facts may be missed if one does not recognize the limited role of the black and white transparencies used in the projectors. Corresponding points on each of the pair of transparencies differed only in the *amount* of light which they transmitted, for they were unselective, i.e. they transmitted any wavelength without discrimination. The physical result of Land's method of projection was simply that the *proportions* of the different wavelengths used in the two projectors varied for different points on the screen. Land found that people can be made to see a wide range of colours by using in the projectors 'any pair of wavelengths that are far enough apart'. He did not, however, claim, as some critics have thought, that all the shades experienced in normal colour vision could be induced by his technique, nor that the latter yielded faithful reproductions of the colours of the objects which had been photographed in black and white. Land's experimental results have been confirmed by other investigators.[10]

Land's results met with considerable incredulity among physicists, who have for centuries been talking of 'red light', 'blue light', etc., as if colours were properties of light of certain wavelengths. It has sometimes been suggested that what Land's subjects were reporting were so-called memory-colours, i.e. that they were ascribing to pictures of familiar kinds of objects their remembered colours. Land adequately ruled out this explanation, e.g. by showing a picture of twelve objects, only one of them of a known colour (an orange). Yet observers were consistent in naming the colours which they saw in the objects in the picture, and these colours corresponded quite well with the colours of the objects which had been photographed in black and white. Land's conclusion was that light waves 'are not in themselves colour making. Rather they are bearers of information that the eye uses to assign appropriate colours to various objects *in an image*.' (My italics.) Though Land does not discuss philosophers' questions, I presume that when he speaks thus of 'images', he conceives such images as being *in us*, as being sense-data in a sense which is not theory-neutral. In any case, surely his data force us to this conclusion.

If readers find it incredible that we can be made to see very different colours by lights of slightly different shades of yellow, they should repeat a simple experiment which Land's data prompted me to try. All that one needs is a set of the fairy lamps used to adorn Christmas trees which contains both light yellow and darker yellow or orange lamps. Stuff the wiring and lighted lamps in a box and close it, leaving one light yellow lamp outside at one corner and one or two of the darker yellow lamps outside at the opposite corner. Make these lights cast two shadows from e.g. a candlestick on to a piece of white paper. You will find that one shadow looks (ph) and looks green, and the other magenta; and these colours can be made fairly vivid by adjusting distances, etc.

In an admirably lucid and balanced appraisal[11] of Land's results, Deane B. Judd has argued that if account is taken of facts about colour-vision which had hitherto been known only to a few specialists, Land's results might have been predicted. (Land has dissented, and this disagreement will have to be resolved by the experts.) The main facts to which Judd was here referring are the results of experiments carried out in the 1930s by Harry Helson, and the principles invoked by Helson and Judd to explain these results.[12] In Helson's earlier experiments, he used 27 subjects trained in classifying colours on a scale which distinguished 16 hues. Each subject had to name the hues he saw when he looked at pieces of by-daylight grey paper illuminated by coloured light. Sixteen different shades of grey paper were used, graded from off-white to off-black. Each of these was viewed in each of four different illuminants, red, yellow, green, and blue. In each illumination, each sample was viewed against three different backgrounds—black, medium grey, and white. The tests were made after the subjects' eyes had been adapted to the illumination in question. The findings were as follows. Some of the samples were seen as grey, namely samples whose reflectance (lightness) was close to that of the background and some were seen as having the colour of the illuminant, namely those whose reflectance was greater than that of the background, *and some were seen as having the colour of the after-image complementary to the colour of the illuminant*, namely those whose reflectance was less than that of the background. For example, in red lighting and with a grey background, the lightest grey samples looked red, some intermediate samples looked grey and the darkest samples looked blue-green (which, as you have verified, is the after-image complementary of red). In his later experiments, Helson found that the same principle held when grey samples were replaced with multicoloured samples. What determined the apparent colour of a sample in coloured light was not its daylight colour, but the *amount* of this light which it reflected. Helson summed up his results thus: 'If we arrange the samples in order of decreasing reflectance [lightness], for each illuminant we find, first, reports of the illuminant hue, . . . secondly, reports of achromaticity [greys] . . . and, thirdly, on grey and white grounds, after-image hues with the darkest samples.'[13]

Helson's data led him and Judd to formulate equations which make it possible to predict fairly accurately the colour which *any* object will look in an illuminant of *any* colour viewed against *any* background; and thereby, they claimed, to give a unified explanation of phenomena which had hitherto been thought to require different mechanisms for their explanation: i.e. of colour-constancy and its limits, of the effects of adaptation, and of simultaneous colour contrast. And Judd has claimed that these equations would enable one to predict the surprising results of Land's experiments, though he admits that he would never have thought of attempting this if Land had not produced his data. *The daylight hues of objects and backgrounds do not figure in the Helson–Judd equations at all.* The key conception is that of 'adaptation reflectance', i.e., roughly, the average *reflectance* of the whole scene to which a person's eyes are currently adapted. Notice the significance of Helson's discovery that paper of any daylight hue may be made to appear either the colour of the illuminant, or grey, *or the colour of the after-image complementary to that of the illuminant.* The colours of after-images, which are visible whether our eyes are open or shut, *must* be generated by the CNS. It is not surprising then that Helson's data led him to conclude that the other colours that we see are no more 'real' than after-image colours.[14]

Many philosophers have endorsed Berkeley's thesis that those arguments which are thought to prove that secondary qualities exist only in the mind would prove the same thing of primary qualities. But this thesis must be disputed. Variation in the phenomenal colours of a thing depends on many factors which do not affect its phenomenal shapes and sizes; and some of these factors pose, for Realism concerning colours, problems which do not arise for Realism concerning primary qualities, notably these factors: the wavelength-composition of the light(s), the relative position(s) of the light-source(s), the reflectance of the object(s) in the background and the strength of the light reflected therefrom, and the state of adaptation of the observer's eyes and brain. Even if we ignored all of these factors except the last, a Selective theory of colour-vision is eliminated thereby. Changes in the observer's CNS can make a thing look$_{(ph)}$ a different colour, even if we interpret the phrase "different in colour" as meaning given different colour-names in English.* Bright *red* is made to fade to a light coral *pink* simply by gazing at it and over-working one's red-making cones. According to the Selective theory, the function of the relevant processes in the CNS is to reveal things and their properties which exist independently of the observer. But the states of his CNS form one of the factors which determine the phenomenal colours of a thing. It is not inconsistent to say that a person's CNS reveals a relational property of a thing like being-round-from this-place; for the terms involved in this relation do not include the CNS of the observer. It would, however, be inconsistent to say

* As Rush Rhees seems to do. See p. 152 below.

that a person's CNS reveals the various colours of a thing and that these are relational properties of that thing; for the terms of the complex relations in question will have to include the states of the observer's eyes and brain. We cannot then claim for colour-vision that the observer's CNS *reveals* qualities which things have independently of being perceived by creatures like us.

We seem to be obliged to conclude that the colours which 'visibly inhere in' physical things are not really inherent *in them*. In that case, we seem to be obliged to choose between the following alternatives:

(i) that the objects which are visibly coloured are sense-data, *qua* transitory by-products of the CNS,

(ii) that many visible objects are surfaces of external physical objects, but that the colour qualities that we see are generated by the CNS and 'projected' on to these objects.

But is the latter position coherent? Can we adopt a Generative theory concerning colours and a selective theory concerning the visible shapes, distances and directions of physical things? This, according to C. D. Broad, is 'what the average person with a scientific training believes'. But consider what Broad has said about this view:

> this muddled mixture of theories is not consistent with itself or with the facts . . . When I look at a penny, the brown colour that I see is seen spread out over the round contour . . . We are asked to believe that there is brownness without shape "in me", and round shape without colour out there where the penny is, and yet that in some mysterious way, the shapeless brownness "in me" is projected into the round contour of the penny "out there". If this be not nonsense I do not know what nonsense is.[15]

The objection is that rejecting Realism regarding colours requires rejection of Realism for vision; and how then can a Realist avoid a complete rout? Yet, as we have seen in chapter 4, there are very strong grounds for rejecting the alternative theories between which we seem obliged to choose if we abandon Realism. Can this dilemma be resolved except by Hume's method, 'carelessness and inattention'?

# 10

# Some Recent Attempts to Sweep the Problems under the Carpet

My present quandary is characteristic of philosophical problems. Arguments which seem irresistible conflict with one's common-sense convictions, and require one to choose between theories which are all hard to believe. According to Wittgenstein, such a dilemma is a symptom of a certain kind of confusion: of one which results from seeking explanations where none should be sought, from borrowing words from everyday language, inventing new rules for their use, and getting entangled in one's own rules. According to Wittgenstein's *Philosophical Investigations* (Oxford, 1953), the panacea for such problems is to observe these precepts:

We must not advance any kind of theory . . . We must do away with all *explanation* and description alone must take its place (109);

Philosophy may in no way interfere with the actual use of language; it can in the end only describe it . . . It leaves everything as it is (124);

Since everything lies open to view there is nothing to explain(126);

In philosophy we do not [presumably he meant 'should not'] draw conclusions . . . Philosophy only states what everyone admits (599);

What we do [i.e. should do] is to bring words back from their metaphysical to their everyday use (116);

Grammar tells what kind of object anything is (373).

One of Wittgenstein's maxims is 'don't think, but look' (66). But what he wanted us to look *at* are our everyday uses of language. He claims that the mistake which had been made by philosophers was to try to explain such uses of language in terms of 'our experiences'

(654–5). If Wittgenstein is right, my approach to the philosophy of perception is all wrong. My maxims have been that we should think not only about verbs like "looks" but about our perceptual experiences, about how things look and look $_{(ph)}$, and that we should ask why things look and look$_{(ph)}$ as they do. Can my present dilemma be solved by following Wittgenstein's precepts? I think that it can thus be *forgotten* or *ignored*, but that this is a way of inducing carelessness and inattention, an alternative to Hume's method of playing backgammon or having a party. Something must be said, however, about Wittgenstein's programme for philosophy, since it has been so influential. Most English-speaking philosophers now equate philosophy with a study of 'concepts', but what they mean by this commonly turns out to be a description of English usage and classification of the practical jobs which we do with words. I shall explain why I reject this conception of the philosopher's function and indicate what I think his function should be. Let us start, however, by asking what, if anything, the kinds of linguistic study inspired by Wittgenstein have contributed to the philosophy of perception.

Its practitioners have shown, and this is easy, that many statements made by philosophers are absurd if interpreted as everyday statements, e.g. that pigs can be seen only 'indirectly' or not 'immediately'. They have helped us to see the arbitrariness of the rules adopted by those who use "sense-datum". A few of them have recently acknowledged 'the phenomenological use' of verbs like "looks", but have not noticed the elasticity of this use, nor always kept it distinct, in their own arguments, from their other uses. Some have reminded us about the kind of contrast which we make in distinguishing between 'real' and 'apparent' perceptible properties, but have not sorted out all the relevant uses of "real". The question which I have been pressing is commonly neglected, namely how can we reconcile with the relevant phenomenological facts our common-sense conviction that so-called secondary qualities, especially colours, are qualities inherent in physical things? Even to ask this question involves treating beliefs enshrined in everyday talk as a theory, as conceivably false; and this is outlawed by Wittgenstein's precepts. A kind of therapy often offered to cure us of asking my question is the emphatic repetition of everyday sentences, like '*of course* tomatoes are red' or 'tomatoes *are* physical objects', or perhaps the remainder that we speak of light *revealing* and darkness *concealing* the colours of things. Philosophers who (unlike myself) have strayed so far as to deny that any perceptual judgements about physical objects are incorrigible, are recalled to sanity by such statements as:

> If I watch for some time an animal a few feet in front of me, in a good light, if I prod it perhaps, and take note of the noises it makes, I may say 'That's a pig'; and . . . nothing could be produced, that would show that I had made a mistake.[1]

Such reminders about everyday usage are monotonous if much repeated. What remains for philosophers who follow Wittgenstein's precepts to say about perception? Not much, unless, in Austin's words, they seek 'amusement' and 'instruction' in 'hounding down the minutiae' of English usage.[2] This explains why so much ink has been spilt debating questions like 'can we see (i.e. is it permissible to speak of 'seeing') what isn't there?' Let us consider Gilbert Ryle's emphatic answer in *The Concept of Mind* 1949. Ryle draws a sharp distinction between our verb "seeing" and his verb " 'seeing' ", between "hearing" and " 'hearing' ", etc. He tells us that our verbs of perception, "see" "hear", etc., 'cover only achievements', 'observational successes' (pp. 222–3). He describes such verbs as 'achievement words'. He writes: 'Just as a person cannot win a race unsuccessfully . . . so a person cannot see incorrectly' (p. 238), that a person 'can only see what is there to be seen and hear only what is there to be heard' (p. 246). Any case where a person is perceptually conscious of something which is not there is to be classified as 'seeing', not seeing, etc. Ryle equates his verb " 'seeing' " with *fancying that* one sees or *seeming* to see or *imagining that* one sees. Ryle interprets "what is there to be seen" very narrowly indeed. Having classified dreaming as 'seeing', not seeing, he says: 'witnessing a public cinematograph show is one way of inducing a certain sort of dreaming.. The spectator there is seeing variously illuminated sheets of linen, but he is 'seeing' rolling prairies' (p. 255).

This example of Ryle's legislation about (apparently intended as description of) English usage is no more remarkable than many others in his book. Consider the implications. What we *see,* when at the cinema or watching TV, are objects of which we are not normally perceptually conscious, linen or glass. We only fancy that we are seeing, for example, astronauts walking on the moon. (This suggests that it is a remarkable coincidence that the things which different members of the audience *imagine that* they are seeing correspond so closely.) Ryle writes as if he wishes so to restrict our use of "see" that its grammatical object must be a description of something tangible as well as visible, e.g. a piece of linen. Why? Presumably because, were we to adopt *his* usage, we should become immune to some of the arguments against Realism. Arguments concerning visual hallucinations and after-image colours could then be dismissed without argument as cases of 'seeing', i.e. of *fancying that* we are seeing things which we are *not* seeing. This method of propping up common sense would have been found less persuasive by his readers if they had recalled something which Ryle forgot when applying his new technical term "achievement word" to "see", "hear", etc.; namely that the relevant category of verbs was to include 'verbs of failure'—"miss" as well as "hit", "drop" as well as "catch" (p. 130). So it should include "misperceive", "mishear", "misread", "mistake for", etc. To Ryle's assertion that 'a person cannot see incorrectly', we should add another grammatical note, that one cannot be said to 'misperceive correctly'.

Anyone who accepts Ryle's thesis that we only fancy that we see after-images, or prairies on cinema screens, has a short way of dismissing some of the facts described in the previous chapter. Land's subjects *saw* only a pice of linen, Helson's earlier subjects *saw* only pieces of grey paper, and when (as *we* say) you saw coloured after-images you only fancied that you saw the various colours. If anyone is tempted thus to sweep the awkward facts under the carpet, he should at least admit that he is not following English usage, which Ryle commonly treats as his court of appeal. Moreover, for anyone who maintains that after-image colours are not seen, but only 'seen', fancied, the implications will be awkward. In my experiment where two yellow lamps cast shadows which are green and magenta, the latter colours are after-image complementaries of each other. But the fact that the shadows look, as well as look$_{(ph)}$, green and magenta is publicly observable, in the senses that people with normal vision agree in naming the colours they see, and that the colours are visibly located out there on the paper. If you sought to dismiss such facts by saying that *shadows* are 'seen' and not seen, this has unacceptable implications. When you look at things in sun-light or lamp-light, a large part of the scene consists of shadows. Is anyone prepared to say that he *sees* only those surfaces of things which are directly illuminated?

Whether we can see (may in English speak of 'seeing') what isn't there has been a burning issue among linguistic philosophers. Those who have affirmed this and those who have denied it are equally dogmatic, though about equally divided. I shall not debate this issue, since no philosophical questions hang on it (unless philosophy is a branch of English grammar). An appropriate answer has been given by Quinton:

> Statements containing verbs of perception are true only if whatever their direct object refers to actually exists *in its proper manner*—tables, clouds, ghosts, noises in the "public world", for everybody; after-images, noises in one's head for the speaker alone (my italics).[3]

But if Ryle's thesis is amended thus, our use of "see" cannot be used to bolster a common sense account of perception. The 'manner' in which colours exist—whether they inhere in tables and clouds, or, like after-images, exist only in us—will still have to be decided by argument.

Philosophers who accept Wittgenstein's principle that grammar tells us what kind of object anything is have drawn many surprising conclusions. According to Rush Rhees, when we say that two things are of the same colour, red, 'the identity, the sameness, comes from the language'.[4] He meant, apparently, that the only sense that we can give to "the same in colour" is 'given the same colour-name in the language' that is, presumably, the language in which one is speaking. But if Rhees had been using his native tongue, Welsh, the adjective applicable to reds ("coch") is applied also to the warmer browns. There are many different ways in which a language may group the millions of colours which its users can discriminate, but the English phrase "same in colour" need not mean 'given the same colour name in English', and the English sentence "This is exactly the same colour as that" does not imply that English has a name for the specific shade in question. Unless we could each recognize resemblances between *colours*, independently of learning to use colour *names*, we could not learn to use any colour names. When we introduce a new colour name, we do not *create* a new resemblance. A person can apply a colour name to certain similar shades only if, independently of associating them with any name, he can recognize the similarity between these shades and their differences from other shades.

One of the most unfortunate results of much recent Anglo-linguistic philosophy is the segregation of philosophy from the sciences. Wittgenstein's precepts are not the only source of this isolationism. G. E. Moore devoted the first half of the twentieth century to the defence of his common-sense convictions, and his method, in practice, consisted in giving complex paraphrases of simple everyday utterances like 'I now see my hand'. For Moore, the world presented no problems. He says in his autobiography 'I do not think that the world or the sciences would ever have suggested to me any philosophical problems'.[5] Ayer wrote in 1936 that the philosopher 'is only concerned with the way in which we speak', that we may 'speak of him loosely as analysing facts, or notions, or even things. But . . . these are simply ways of saying that he is concerned with the definition of the corresponding words'.[6] Ayer did not, however, advocate that philosophers should ignore words used by scientists. Restriction of the philosopher's subject-matter to *everyday* language was due to Moore's example and Wittgenstein's precepts. These gave birth to a view, expressed by Norman Malcolm, that 'it is not possible for an ordinary form of speech to be improper. That is to say, ordinary language is correct language.'[7] Wittgenstein's principle that Grammar tells us what things are like led philosophers to seek understanding of the world by inspecting the ways in which people who are ignorant about philosophy and science talk about the world. Hence the situation, recorded by Warnock in 1958, in the course of *defending* linguistic philosophy, that many contemporary philosophers 'would say . . . that philosophy is the study of the concepts that we employ, *and not of the facts, phenomena, cases, or events to which those concepts might be or are applied*' (my italics).[8] As this statement indicates, what had, for many, been excluded from philosophy includes all empirical facts except grammatical facts. In two recent books,[9] Warnock acknowledges how fruitless such philosophy has been, but his proposed remedy is more research into our concepts, i.e. word-uses. Wittgenstein's precepts would justify a philosopher who is discussing perception in dismissing phenomenological variability with the remark that *of course* (we say that) things look different in different circumstances, and in ignoring as philosophically irrelevant, because not expressed in everyday language, what scientists have discovered about perception. Or, if any heed is to be paid to what scientists say, it will be to the *words* they use, like "colour-blindness' or "shape-constancy", whose meanings will be taken at their face-value without attention to the relevant facts.

The philosopher whose work complies most closely with Wittgenstein's precepts is J. L. Austin. The subtlety and wit with which he has described how well-educated Englishmen talk when talking very carefully has done much to popularize this pursuit. Moreover, he offered a rationale which makes this method sound less unexciting than do Wittgenstein's precepts. He proposed that the term "linguistic philosophy" be replaced by "linguistic phenomenology", and the reason he offered for choosing this phrase was:

> When we examine what we should say when, what words we should use in what situations, we are looking again not *merely* at words . . . but also at the realities we use the words to talk about: we are using a sharpened awareness of words to sharpen our perception of, though not as the final arbiter, of the phenomena.[10]

This *sounds* promising. A person's perception of something may indeed be sharpened by his learning or inventing some *new* way of describing it. But in practice, the method whereby Austin sought to sharpen our perception is the one commended by Wittgenstein—reminding us of the familiar ways in which we do, normally, describe them, of the uses of English which we learnt at our mothers' knees. Surely this is like trying to improve one's vision by donning spectacles which lack lenses.

Admittedly Austin did sharpen our perception *of English grammar*. Like Ryle, he invented new technical terms for describing the functions of certain words and sentences, but never for redescribing the (other) realities or phenomena which we use words to talk about. *Sense and Sensibilia* is a posthumously published book, reconstructed by Warnock from Austin's notes for a course of lectures on perception. In this book, Austin warns us against 'tampering' with our mother-tongue.[11] Apart from double vision, he found nothing in the least puzzling about any of the phenomena or the realities. Like Moore, it is only things said by philosophers which he found puzzling. He by-passed all questions about what is real, in the existential sense, by focusing on a different function of "real"—that in which "real" is 'substantive-hungry' (§ VII). He failed to distinguish this use from the one, so important in the language of perception, in which "real" is contrasted with "apparent" and is attached to the name of some kind of perceptible property. He discussed certain verbs which play important roles in the language of perception—"look", "appear", and "seem" (§ IV). But his discussion obscures rather than clarifies the distinction which I take to be of cardinal importance—between their phenomenological use and their use in giving estimates of the properties of perceived objects. This major difference of function was left blurred as a result of Austin's preoccupation with 'the minuter differences' (p. 36), with grammatical constructions which are of no philosophical interest (pp. 34–9), and with the obvious point that "looks", "appears", and "seems" are not interchangeable in many contexts (p. 33). His grammatical enquiries were intended to illuminate what other philosophers had written about perception, but he often failed to see the wood for the trees. The closest that he came to discussing the classical problems concerning primary and secondary qualities was in criticizing the thesis that "the real colour of a thing" means 'the colour it looks to a normal observer in . . . normal or standard illumination' (pp. 65–6). He rejects this account on the ground that it is not what we mean when we say of a woman with dyed hair 'That isn't the real colour of her hair'! And by asking questions like 'What is the real colour of the sky? Of the sun? Of the moon?' This shows that our common convention for using "the real colour of" is inapplicable in some cases. Then what did Austin wish to put in its place? There is no hint of an answer. But the most serious gap in Austin's lectures on perception is his failure to mention the data or language or theories of the scientists who study perception.

The defects of this flippant and amusing book have been stressed because it has been seriously regarded as disposing of the traditional problems about perception. Had these problems been due solely to philosophers 'tampering' with their mother-tongues, Austin's medicine might have been effective. But the most intractable problems concerning perception arise from: (*a*) phenomenological facts which are rarely noticed by the average practical man, and (*b*) conflicts between the 'conceptual schemes' of scientists and those which are enshrined in our everyday dictions, which reflect many of the beliefs of our prescientific ancestors. I find it surprising that a thinker as acute as Austin should think that problems which arise largely from scientific discoveries can be solved by reminding us how people talk when oblivious to, or not discussing, such problems, when they are using blunt multi-purpose tools provided by a natural language which has slowly evolved to meet men's practical needs.

Austin's statements about grammar are usually accurate, at any rate for the talk of the few people as scrupulous as himself. (Oddly enough, it is *their* talk which he called *ordinary* language.) But linguistic philosophers very often make false statements about English usage in the interests of some theory or thesis. As Ayer himself has pointed out,[12] their theses can often be traced to an unacknowledged application of some form of 'the' verification principle. This suggests that the linguistic philosophers in question do not wish to abandon traditional British Empiricism, of whose main thesis Ayer's verification principle purported to be an up-to-date formulation. As traditionally interpreted, however, Empiricism is *not* the thesis that all knowledge is based on incorrigible statements. That thesis is a legacy from the main rival theory of knowledge, Rationalism. Traditional British Empiricism claims that no knowledge about the world is 'innate', or grasped by intuition as *self*-evident, that all such knowledge is based upon data yielded by our sense-organs or by self-awareness. Why on earth should a philosopher who accepts this thesis ignore all empirical facts except facts about everyday language; or confuse this thesis with some *ad hoc* rule designed for identifying meaningless sentences? The arguments used by linguistic philosophers show that they are, sometimes, still concerned with the theory of knowledge, with questions concerning the *justification* of claims to have knowledge. In that case, they ought surely to be interested in all knowledge and the methods of getting it. For 2,500 years the philosopher's main goal had been to construct a theory, world-view, 'metaphysical system', or 'conceptual scheme', whose purpose was, *not* to describe and classify current uses of his native tongue, but to fit and make sense of the non-linguistic facts, i.e. what was currently known or believed about the world and ourselves. Not surprisingly, they sometimes departed from the conventions of everyday language and introduced technical terms.

Philosophers who confine their attention to knowledge so ancient that it has become embalmed in the English of Everyman are gratuitously decimating their subject-matter. Before Wittgenstein wrote in his first book 'All philosophy is critique of language',[13] no important philosopher would have accepted this restricted conception of his subject. The conception of philosophy which I have been trying to apply in this book is a natural corollary of Empiricism. It is the view that a philosopher should take into account all relevant empirical facts and that his goal is to try to render the facts intelligible. In this respect, the philosopher's goal coincides with *one* of the scientist's goals. Scientists are not solely concerned to discover laws in accordance with which events *do in fact* happen. They seek also to explain why the laws are as they are. I conclude that Anglo-linguistic philosophy* has been an aberration; and that it is a way of sweeping under the carpet problems about the phenomena and the realities.

I shall now review another procedure which should, I think, be described as a way of concealing problems concerning perception. In general terms, it consists of identifying our perceptual experiences or their contents with things of an entirely different nature. This may be done by a definitional decree, a method pioneered by Thomas Hobbes in the seventeenth century, or simply by *asserting* that something is identical with something else. Philosophical Behaviourism is one manifestation of this method. For psychologists, Behaviourism originated as a methodological principle or policy—not to rely upon 'introspective reports', to accept as hard facts what has been observed and is publicly observable, i.e. the overt behaviour of rats, pigeons, or people. In philosophy, Behaviourism usually takes the form of a thesis about the meanings of expressions which describe what we call 'states of mind', e.g. that statements containing such expressions can be completely 'analysed' in terms of statements about overt behaviour.[14] The main motive for adopting such a thesis has, I think, been acceptance of 'the' verification principle. In 1936, Ayer embraced a behaviouristic account of statements about *other* people's 'experiences', on the ground that 'their experiences are completely inaccessible to *my* observation' (my italics).[15] As his argument shows, Ayer's premise was that a statement is meaningful *for me*, if and only if it is verifiable by me, *and* is verifiable by me only if *I* can observe what the statement is about. Ayer was not, however,

* In another book, *A Critique of Linguistic Philosophy*, Oxford, 1970, I have stressed and illustrated the differences between various forms of Anglo-linguistic philosophy. In its now most common forms, it is conducted in jargon which is usually not explained, notably "the concept of", "the logic of the concept", "category", and "criterion".

a Behaviourist concerning his own experiences, and was, therefore, in the uncomfortable position of having, for example, to interpret "pain" very differently in 'John has a pain' and in 'I have a pain'. The former, on Ayer's account, is about the speaker's visual and auditory sense-data when he watches John wince, hears him howl, etc. Whereas 'I have a pain' is about *a pain*. Thorough-going Behaviourism requires that one should ignore oneself or pretend to be unconscious, and Ayer was never willing to do this. The plausibility of behaviouristic analyses varies for different words. It is plausible for "ambitious" or "obstinate", fairly plausible for "afraid" or "angry", very implausible for "pain", and even more implausible for words like "see", "recognize" or "red". J. J. C. Smart has, however, offered a behaviouristic account of the meanings of colour-words and, by implication, of "see".[16]

Smart writes:

> As against the common view that colour words must be meaningless to the congenitally blind, I would rather say . . . that the congenitally blind could in fact understand the meanings of colour words every bit as well as sighted people can.

Smart's defence of this thesis involves defining "a normal human percipient" thus: 'a person A is more normal than a person B with respect to a certain type of *colour discrimination* if he can discriminate things of a certain sort with respect to *colour* while B cannot do so' (my italics). (As Smart admits, there may, on this definition, be no normal percipient, since A might be the best human discriminator of reds, B of blues.) Now Smart's definition uses "colour" twice. How is a congenitally blind man to understand what Smart is talking *about*? Smart tries to answer this by asking us to envisage a blind ruler doing experiments on his sighted slaves. This project is made to appear possible by describing it in two stages, and not mentioning the blindness of the experimenter until stage two. In the first stage, the experiments are to be conducted by 'You'. 'You' are to tell the slaves to sort samples of wool into bundles which '*appear* to differ in some obvious way'; and are to ensure that the samples differ only in *hue* and not in their *brightness or darkness* or (*visible*) *texture*; and 'You' are to vary the *colour* of the *light*, in order to find if this affects the slaves' 'discriminatory reactions'! The aim of this experiment was apparently to enable a congenitally blind experimenter to understand what "colour" means. Can anyone think of an experiment which will enable the poor blind man to understand the use of "colour", "light", "brightness", "darkness", etc., in Smart's experimental instructions?

No doubt a congenitally blind ruler could find that his slaves consistently react differently to things which he cannot discriminate, and could infer that they experience sensible qualities which he does not, and could use a slave as a colour-meter for distinguishing ripe and unripe tomatoes, etc. But for him, the words used by his slaves to refer to such sensible qualities would refer to something-I-know-not-what. Notice the ambiguity of "discriminate" which helps to conceal the inconsistencies of Behaviourism. In its primary use, "to discriminate" means to perceive, be aware of, a difference. According to the behaviourist programme—to define words applicable to states of mind in terms of what you can observe others doing—"to discriminate" must mean 'to behave differently towards'. You will have observed that other people do react differently to things which you see to be of different colours. Their behaviour would be mysterious unless you assume (as we all do) that other people discriminate colours in the sense in which you do, i.e. seeing, being conscious of, different qualities in different directions. To be a consistent behaviourist and pretend that one is unconscious is an incoherent position. Nobody could observe other people's discriminatory reactions without being *conscious* of qualitative differences between different colours, between different sounds, etc.

Smart's behaviouristic account of colour words is not, however, his last word. He says that it is 'not *quite* true that our inner experiences do not matter at all for the analysis of our colour concepts', since it is conceivable that the colours of everything might suddenly change in some systematic way while everyone's discriminatory behaviour remained unchanged. So he concedes that we do have 'inner experiences' or 'sense-data', but says that these are unimportant; and in Chapter V he employs a different method for sweeping away problems concerning perception. This is to assert that 'immediate experiences', etc., *are* brain processes. This assertion of identity is not presented as being true by definition but as being 'factual and contingent', like the identification of lightning with a movement of electrical charges from a cloud to the earth. (On Smart's premises lighting is identical with thunder, which seems odd.) If Smart had merely claimed that the immediate and sufficient cause of an immediate experience or sense-datum is a brain process, this would be an intelligible way of formulating Physicalism, and of dispensing with minds conceived as immaterial substances. Smart wishes, however, to sweep out of sight the sensible qualities which we experience. His reasons are that 'we [we physicists?] expect the ultimate laws of nature to relate to simple or at least homogeneous entities' (like the laws of mechanics, presumably), and that causal laws relating 'experiences' to 'neurophysiological processes involving billions of neurons' would not be conveniently simple (p. 90). So he just *asserts* that immediate experiences and their contents *are* brain-processes. I shall mention only one of the many problems which confront Smart. The data of our sense-experience (whether or not we call it 'immediate') have qualities not possessed by brain processes. When one sees something which looks yellow, the causally relevant brain processes are not yellow, so what is it that *is* yellow? Smart says that what he is identifying with a brain process is not the sense-datum or after-image but the *process*: having-a-sense-datum or having-an-after image. But this does not answer the question 'what is yellow?', which Smart refrains from asking. To stop us from asking it, Smart should not have conceded that his behaviouristic account of colour words is 'not *quite* true'. He should have pretended that he (and we) cannot *discriminate* colours in the first person use of this verb. Then the need to identify the having of sense-data and after-images with brain processes does not arise. Though if people were not conscious of colour-qualities, sound-qualities, etc., physics could not have arisen either, nor *homo sapiens*.

Smart wishes to identify immediate experiences and sense-data with *physical* processes. He could not do this in any simple manner, because he was acquainted with the science of vision. Philosophers who are not sometimes offer much simpler solutions concerning secondary qualities; e.g. that sound-qualities *are* mechanical vibrations, that thermal qualities *are* motions of corpuscles, that colours *are* light-waves of certain wavelengths. D. Williams has argued[17] that 'if colors are not physical and colors exist, then it is false that everything is physical'; and that Physicalism may be defended by saying: 'an experienced colour quale . . . is literally identical with the chronogeometrical structure which is its physical condition', or, more simply, identical with 'a vibrational frequency'; and that 'the color red can literally be constituted out of pattern elements none of which is red'. This route is barred, however, by the fact that one can be made to see any colour by light-stimuli having any of an infinite variety of different mixtures of wavelengths. In any case, this crude kind of Physicalism is incongruous for reasons given by Berkeley in his *First Dialogue*. He pointed out that if 'sound in the real sense' is 'nothing but a certain motion in the air', it follows that 'real sounds may possibly be *seen* or *felt* but never *heard*'. (And if thermal sense-qualities *are* motions, warmth is, in principle, visible; and so on). We can see and feel the vibrations of a bell or organ, but does this reveal the real nature of the *sounds* which they make us *hear*?

Another gambit of the kind which we are considering is to 'identify' secondary qualities with causal powers possessed by external objects. Ascribing redness, for example, to physical objects implies that these objects have the causal power to make us (most of us) see red(s). (This statement can be accepted by realists as well as representationalists, though an Austin might wish us to delete as redundant the words "have the causal power to".) But this causal power cannot be *identified* with the colour qualities in question, for the power is specified by a description within which "red(s)" is used to refer to such qualities. Could this causal power be specified without so using "red(s)"? Scientists might do so thus: the causal power of reflecting, in daylight or its equivalent, one or other of the infinite number of different wavelength mixtures which have the causal power to stimulate the different types of cones in a normal human eye in some ratio in the following range.... However, "red" can be omitted from such a description only if, and because, it has been independently established that stimulation of a person's eyes in certain ways makes him *see* red(s), i.e. colour-qualities which he calls 'red'. The complex causal property just described is not the sort of thing which could be seen, however hard one stared at things like ripe tomatoes. The short description of this causal property given in the second sentence of this paragraph is simple because it is incomplete. It ceases to be simple if we try so to formulate it that, in the present sense of "having a colour", the same physical surface is not to have a host of colours. In many conditions white material makes us see colours other than white, and indeed it can make us see nearly all of the colours we can see.

Another way of trying to sweep out of sight certain problems about perception is found in chapter 7 of D. M. Armstrong's *Perception and the Physical World* (London, 1961). In effect, Armstrong identifies sense-data ('sense-impressions') with beliefs. His arguments are hard to follow for various reasons. He argues as if it is only in cases of 'sensory illusions' that we have occasion for describing sense-impressions (for what I call 'phenomenal descriptions'). He argues as if verbs like "looks" are only used to express estimates about physical objects (p. 92). However, consider some of the things he says. He admits that when a person is subject to a visual illusion, he is disposed to say 'there is an object in my visual field which no attempted analysis . . . can conjure away'. But to say this, he says, is 'completely mistaken'.

> What we are asserting is . . . that when (or in so far as) we suffer from sensory illusion, there is no object at all, physical or non-physical, which we are perceiving in any possible sense of the word 'perceiving'. There is simply the (completely) false belief that ordinary perceiving is taking place (p. 83).

This is amended so that "false belief" includes 'inclination to [accept] a false belief' (p. 87). Then what about what others would describe as 'the perceptual experience or sense-impression on which this belief is founded'? Armstrong proceeds to identify a person's visual sense-impression with 'his false belief . . . that he sees a thing of a certain colour and shape' (p. 88); and he then supports this thesis by claiming that words like "red" and "oval" are used in different senses when applied to physical objects and 'when we use them to describe sense-impressions' (p. 91). In their latter use, there is, on Armstrong's account, nothing for them to apply to except false beliefs, though it seems odd to describe a *belief* as red or oval. And if such adjectives apply to false beliefs in reports of sensory illusions, should they not apply to true beliefs in other perceptual reports? Armstrong is claiming (if I have understood him) that "red" is used in different senses when applied to a ripe tomato and to something which turns out not to be red. This has unacceptable implications. In Helson's experiments, his subjects did not know the real (daylight) colours of the papers whose apparent colours they were asked to name. Unless we assume that people can recognize colours as such, can apply "red" consistently and in the same sense independently of knowing the 'real' colours of the things they are looking at, Helson's experiments would be pointless; and

Land's; and Newton's; and experiments on 'colour-constancy'. Indeed the possibility of a scientific investigation of colour vision would be undermined. As readers may have guessed, Armstrong accepts Ryle's rigid restriction on the use of verbs like "perceive" and "see".

We have surveyed attempts to dispose of problems concerning our awareness of secondary qualities by identifying this with something else: overt behaviour, brain processes, wave-movements, causal powers or beliefs. These attempts seem to involve a kind of make-believe, a kind which is inconsistent with Empiricism. According to Empiricism, all of our knowledge about physical things is derived from facts ascertained by sense-experience or self-awareness. But unless we were aware of a variety of secondary qualities, nothing could be perceived (unless by so-called extra-sensory perception). We could not, by vision, distinguish different objects unless we saw different colours in different directions, nor detect things by hearing unless we heard a variety of discriminable sound-qualities. To conjure away consciousness of secondary qualities is to throw the baby out with the bath water. If the intention is not to deny the reality of such sense-experiences but to claim that they turn out to be identical with something completely different, such a thesis still involves a kind of conjuring. For surely it is playing tricks with "identical" to assert that e.g. seeing yellow is *identical* either with physical processes which may cause such sense-experience, or with bodily movements which may be caused by it.

# 11
# A Tentative Verdict

IF an introduction to the philosophy of perception ended with some simple solution of the problems which it had been elaborating, this might defeat its purpose, namely to start and not stop thought. Perhaps it is fortunate that I cannot defend all of the features of common-sense Realism, and that my method of salvaging all that I can will be controversial. It should be clear from what has already been said that I think that Realism regarding colour-qualities is ruled out by the phenomenological facts. This requires me to amend, but not, I think, to abandon, Realism. Some philosophers would argue thus: that if we concede that some sensible qualities are generated by the CNS, we must, to be consistent, conclude that all are and that we must then reject the Realism of common sense in favour of one of the alternative theories, among which is what Smart calls 'Scientific Realism'. I think that this is to throw in the towel too readily. A theory of *perception* must take account of senses other than *vision*.

Most philosophical theories of perception have been based primarily upon conclusions concerning vision. I too have been preoccupied with vision, because it poses the main problems; and because, if we compare the information yielded by our eyes with that yielded by our other senses, the former is enormously richer, more detailed and, in terms of the distances of things perceived thereby, more far-ranging. Moreover, so much of our thinking is done in visual terms; meaning by this not merely that for many people thinking is commonly accompanied and illustrated by pictures in the mind's eye, but that in thinking of a physical object, e.g. one's house, people tend to think primarily of its *visible* properties and to locate it in terms of a more or less schematic *pictorial* map. One must, however, beware of the temptation to assume that the contents of everyone else's consciousness are like one's own; that, as Thomas Hobbes put it, 'whosoever looketh into himself . . . shall thereby read and know what are the thoughts and passions [and sense-data] of all other men, upon like occasions'.[1] Many errors have been made by proceeding on this premise. For example, Berkeley and Hume argued as if everyone does all his thinking in, or with, visual images, as they presumably did. Phenomenology is a solitary science. Each of us has to do it for himself. Nevertheless I feel some confidence in surmising that other people are like myself in these respects: that whenever they are awake, they are continuously aware of their own bodies as three-dimensional solids, and of the changing postures thereof; and that they will agree that no knowledge could be more immediate or direct.

One of the besetting sins of philosophers is a preference for the most general of generalizations about the most abstract of abstractions. They usually write as if a theory of perception must be about *perception as such,* as if it can ignore the differences between different modes of perception. But why, for example, should anyone assume that the same account must be given for proprio-perception, i.e. perception of one's own body and its states, and for the perception of external things? Let us, for a change, adopt the maxim 'Don't look, think.' The conceptual scheme of physics (and of current common sense?) requires that, from* any external object which is perceived, there must pass some form of physical energy which alters the state of one's body, and that the latter change mediates one's perception of the external object. This way of thinking suggests that we should adopt a Representative theory for perception of *external* objects, but need not do so for proprio-perception. Though Berkeley did not present it in this way, or with this rationale, the theory of perception outlined in his youthful *Essay* conforms with this principle; though it contains some features which a would-be Realist should reject. Let us explore the principle just suggested to find how far it need take us from the Realism of common sense.

When we are using any of our sense-organs we are usually perceptually conscious of external objects. But if we adopt the phenomenological attitude and consider what is sense-given, some species

* From *or to,* in the case of touching something colder than one's skin.

of sense-data are, and some are not, located in one's own body. The data of vision and of hearing are not. The data of sight are given as occupying determinate places in a three-dimensional field of view. Sounds are usually given as being in (coming from) more or less definite directions, but they are not things of a sort which can *occupy* places. Even what is called a 'singing in one's ears' is not, I find, literally located *in* my ears, or in any specific place.* It is incongruous to say that all of our sense-data exist 'in us', since, at the phenomenological level, this is plainly false for two species of sense-data. But the data of our other senses are located in our own bodies. Admittedly, smelling (like hearing) often involves perceptual consciousness of some external thing, e.g. a dog. But whereas sounds are not literally located in one's ears, smells are literally located within or behind one's nose. I have suggested, in chapter 5, that a similar account should be given regarding the data of the senses of taste and touch. If this is accepted for touch, it must, presumably, be accepted for taste, since tasting involves touching. Would anyone deny that the flavour-qualities which he experiences are located inside his mouth? Or that the various qualities of tactual data—thermal, textural, prickly, tickly, etc.—are located in areas of one's skin? The human skin is not an efficient instrument for measuring the temperature of *external* objects. When iron feels colder than wood to the same hand, we cannot conclude that it *is* colder than the wood; but we may claim to know that the skin now touching the iron is colder than it was when touching the wood. Sensations of touch, taste, and smell are located in our bodies just as erotic sensations are. We are not (or rarely) tempted to ascribe the qualities of the latter to the person's skin, contact with which induces them in or under one's own skin. (Partly because such sensations also occur without such contact; partly because the concomitance between such sensations and such contact is less reliable than that between sucking sugar and experiencing the sensible quality which one calls 'sweet'.) If Realism is expressed by claiming that secondary qualities inhere in physical objects, can one be a Realist regarding the secondary qualities of touch, taste, and smell, on the ground that these do inhere in regions of physical bodies, our bodies, thereby enabling us to identify the types of external objects which cause these experiences.

* I do, however, hear some of the sounds *between* my ears when listening with earphones to stereophonic recordings.

Some Anglo-linguistic philosophers may not be happy about defending Realism thus. They may wish to insist that (we say that) *sugar* is sweet, this *tea* is hot, the *whole harbour* stinks of fish, etc. But surely we need not think with the vulgar to the extent of taking every everyday diction as philosophically final. No consistent theory of perception can be established by reminding us about everyday usage. So far as smell and hearing are concerned, everyday language oscillates between that of Naïve Realism and that of Representationalism. We speak indifferently of things *having* smells and *making* smells, *being* noisy and *making* noises. Those who adopt Ryle's rule that you can only smell or hear what is there to be smelt or heard have to admit that the accusatives for these verbs include "a smell" as well as "a fox", "a noise" as well as "Big Ben". When we say that the tea is hot and sweet, I suggest that all that we should, on reflection, mean by this is that when the tea is brought into contact with the appropriate organs of a normal percipient, it makes him experience, in those organs, certain sensible qualities. Everyday language often provides brief ways of saying things which take more time to say explicitly. When a region of one's body is pervaded by some secondary quality, we describe this as 'having a sensation'. And so it is very strained to speak, as some philosophers have, of 'visual' or 'auditory sensations'. Sound-qualities do not pervade our ears, nor colours our eyes, in the way that flavours pervade our palates, thermal qualities patches of our skin, etc.

If our concern is to defend Realism as distinct from the idiosyncrasies of English grammar, we are free to adopt the following position. Although, for brevity, we talk as if they are qualities of *external* objects, the secondary qualities of touch, taste, and smell inhere in the body of the percipient. This is a physical object, and "inhere in" here means literally 'are located in'. Such secondary qualities 'belong' to *external* things only in the sense that the latter have the power to cause us to experience the former located in appropriate parts of our bodies. Sounds do not, in this sense, inhere in any physical object, not even in *our* bodies. A sound 'belongs' to an external object only in the sense that the latter is its source. And the direction in which a sound is heard is often not the direction of its source. When sound-waves travel down a city street and reach a cross-road, they turn *all* the corners and travel down *each* of the other streets.

The position which I have outlined so far—that most species of secondary qualities inhere in the bodies of percipients—removes the temptation to throw the baby out with the bath water by 'identifying' secondary qualities with abstract entities of some entirely different description. The position outlined cannot be described simply as Realist or simply as Representationalist. It is Realist regarding the ascription of certain species of secondary qualities to certain physical objects, percipients' bodies. It gives a Representationalist account of the ascription of *all* secondary qualities to *external* bodies. We should, however, be abandoning, not amending, Realism if we did not insist that the so-called primary qualities 'inhere in' external bodies as well as in the bodies of percipients. At first sight, it may appear to be inconsistent to claim that, when I handle a match-box, the secondary qualities of touch inhere in my fingers, but not in the match-box, but that the primary qualities inhere both in my fingers and in the match-box. This would, however, be inconsistent only if we pretended not to know that a so-called tactual sensation is in part of one's own skin *in contact with* another body. But we do know this. We learnt it as infants—by touching parts of one's own skin with other parts of it.

It is now time to stop using "primary qualities" uncritically. Philosophers have misused the word "quality" in applying it to the features of things traditionally called 'primary qualities', e.g. shape, size, position, motion, and even number. Consider *number*. Having five fingers is a property of my hand. But so is its property of being *one* hand, and its property of comprising *sixteen* independently movable parts. Number is not a quality (never mind a sensible quality) of things, but an answer to the question 'how many things?'—a question which is vacuous unless we know what are to be counted: fingers, joints, cells? Consider *position*. The present position of my hand is a property of my hand, but it is a *relational* property, a way of referring to the spatial relationships between my hand and other physical objects, e.g. my torso or my table. The *size* of my hand is also a relational property, involving comparison of it with e.g. other people's hands, or a measuring tape. And *motion* is obviously a relational property. Of the so-called primary qualities, the *shape* of a thing is the only property which does not obviously involve spatial relationships between different physical objects. One is inclined to say that the shape of this hand involves only spatial relationships between the several parts of this hand, that this hand would still have a determinate shape even if nothing else existed. But notice that saying this involves treating the hand both as *one* physical object and as a collection of *many* joints. A hand can also be conceived to move, or be moved, though we suppose that nothing exists except it and God who makes the fingers flex. Then its motion would consist in different parts of the hand changing in their spatial relationships to each other. The point of all this is to stress that these so-called primary qualities presuppose a plurality of three-dimensional solids, whether or not these are contiguous like the parts of my hand. The same goes for the other properties which have been classified as primary qualities, e.g. hardness of impenetrability. "M is hard" means, roughly, that M is not easily bent or squashed *by other physical objects*; "M is impenetrable" that *other physical objects* cannot pass through M without displacing its parts. It should now be obvious how preposterous was Locke's procedure—lumping together, as simple qualities, colours and 'solidity', saying that colours inhere in 'solid extended parts', then asking what solidity inheres in, and answering: in something he knew not what. The terms which philosophers have classified as names of primary qualities are ways of talking about the spatial relationships between three-dimensional solids, e.g. between the different parts of one's own body, the only three-dimensional solid with which a person is acquainted 'from the inside'. (If anyone feels that I have, in this paragraph, begged the question by presupposing that position, shape, etc., are attributes of *physical* things, let him survey the writings of philosophers whose theories require them to treat so-called primary qualities as attributes of two-dimensional sense-data. Did any of them succeed, or even recognize the difficulties confronting them? And could the difficulties be solved?)

Imagine a sentient intelligent creature who is like us, except that he lacks four of the traditional five senses, lacks sight, hearing, taste, and smell. If the care of others enabled him to survive to maturity, he would have become familiar with all of the properties of things which have traditionally been called 'primary qualities'. Perception of his own body and of its changing contacts with other bodies would make this possible. (Whether he could learn or invent a language for describing what he could discriminate is another question.) This indicates that if "the sense of touch" is to include all perception not attributable to the other four senses, it must include a great deal more than what philosophers refer to as 'tactual sense-data', which are usually described in language like that used of visual sense-data. The latter are spoken of as 'patches' or 'expanses' pervaded by colour-qualities, tactual sense-data as 'patches' or 'expanses' pervaded by other qualities, thermal or textural or 'prement'. Price speaks of 'a prement expanse' to describe the sense-datum whereby one is aware of a pressure on one's skin. But surely no one not wholly paralysed since birth would describe such pressures simply as sense-*given* qualities. Awareness of pressures on one's skin is so often the result of *exerting* pressure, when pulling, pushing or manipulating things. If "the sense of touch" is to include all that is left if we subtract the other traditional senses, it must include much more than tactual sense-data, however these are described. When, in the dark, one puts on one's shoes and ties the laces 'by touch', one is continuously aware of the changing posture of one's whole body. And aware of *moving*, not merely of movements taking place. For there is a world of difference between moving one's arm and feeling it move, between throwing oneself on the ground and falling. One is aware of oneself as a corporeal *agent*. One's controlled movements involve and depend upon continuous awareness of the relative positions of all the independently movable parts of one's body. (Scientists tell us that the sense-organs upon which this knowledge primarily depends are located in the joints between our bones, and that they record the angles between the bones.[3] This is something that we should never have guessed from introspection. We are not aware of a distinctive sensible quality in our joints varying according to the angles of the bones.) Our imaginary human percipient who lacked four of the five traditional senses could learn to perceive a great deal. Apart from proprio-perception, he could perceive the shapes, sizes, and positions of many external bodies which were not too big or too small to be explored by his own; and could perceive many of their physical properties, not only their (relative) temperatures, their textures, their hardness or softness, but also their weights, their elasticity, and the force of the gale, the acceleration of the bus, etc. Indeed, his conception of a physical object would surely be essentially the same as ours. Should we not then conclude that sight, hearing, taste, and smell are luxuries so far as forming our conception of a physical object is concerned? On the other hand, could a creature possessing *only* these four forms of perception acquire *our* conception of a physical object? I think not.

Our imaginary percipient who lacks vision and hearing, taste and smell would not be tempted to adopt any sense-datum theory of perception. He would be deprived of four senses all of whose data are transitory. Admittedly *some* of his data would be transitory, e.g. tactual sensations. But for him the tactual shapes of pennies would not be subject to phenomenal variation in the way that their looks$_{(ph)}$ are for us, or at least not to anything like the same extent. Admittedly a penny would feel bigger to his tongue than to the palm of his hand, but to his hand which transports the penny first to his tongue and then to the palm of his other hand, the penny is of a constant size. Our imaginary percipient would not be tempted, because some of his sense-data, e.g. tactual sensations and pains, come and go, to infer that he is aware of nothing but transitory sense-data. For his attention would be so much occupied with a three-dimensional solid of which he was aware whenever conscious, his own body. Philosophers fortunately equipped with four more senses have, when not preoccupied with words, been so preoccupied with vision, and to a lesser extent hearing, that they have often forgotten their own bodies, and have written as if perception *is* perception of *external* objects. Like John Locke and Don Locke,[4] and indeed Ayer who makes only a rare passing reference to 'organic sensations'.

Let us turn now to vision. This is where the shoe pinches. The position which we are exploring is Realism regarding (i) perception of one's own body and its states, including states of being pervaded by certain secondary qualities, and (ii) the spatial properties of external objects, which properties can, in many cases, be detected by touch and locomotion. But it involves Representationalism regarding hearing and vision. In the case of hearing this does no violence to common sense. Surely all would agree that hearing the sounds that a thing makes gives one only indirect knowledge about it; that the sounds represent but do not remotely resemble the relevant physical property of the thing, a vibratory motion; and that it is a contingent fact that the things which we can recognize by hearing make us hear the distinctive sounds which make such recognition possible. But it is extremely paradoxical to offer a parallel account of vision. Let us consider Berkeley's *Essay*, in which he tried to mitigate the paradoxes in maintaining that everything that we see is in us, 'in the mind'.

It is not clear to me that in his *Essay* Berkeley was advocating the view which I am exploring, namely that visual sense-data represents *physical objects located in a single space*. In his *Principles* (XLIV) Berkeley says that he had, in the *Essay*, spoken of tangible objects existing 'without the mind', because his earlier purpose did not require him to correct this 'vulgar error'; implying that even then his real view had been the one which he presented later—that *esse* is *percipi* for everything except minds. And Berkeley's language in the *Essay* is ambivalent. Sometimes he speaks of 'tangible objects' existing in 'circumambient space'. But just as often he uses language which fits his later philosophy, and speaks of 'tangible ideas', i.e. tactual sense-data; and he usually does this when formulating his main thesis—that 'visible ideas' represent 'tangible ideas' or 'combinations of tangible ideas'. He is, however, consistent in using Realist language when speaking of his own body. He says, for example, that a person who looks at the moon sees a 'small, round, luminous flat', which 'only suggests to his understanding, that after having passed a certain distance, *to be measured by the motion of his body, which is perceivable by touch*, he shall come to perceive such and such tangible ideas' (XLIV and XLV; my italics).

Berkeley's discussion is of interest here because much of it is relevant to my present concern, to consider whether we can reconcile with Realism a Representative theory of vision. In some respects Berkeley did mitigate the paradoxes of the latter theory, in some respects he embraced gratuitous paradoxes. He was doing the latter when he said 'there is no resemblance between the ideas of sight and things tangible'. Berkeley's thesis is that the only connection there is between what you see when you look at a ball and what you feel when you touch it is the sort of connection there is between the inscription "ball" and balls. This analogy is used by Berkeley to explain how we come to identify, mistakenly he thinks, a certain 'visible shape' and a certain 'tangible shape', how we come to apply the same words to each, e.g. "shape", and more specifically "round". Berkeley's explanation is that certain similar patterns of colour have so often been experienced concurrently with certain kinds of tactual sensations that the former automatically make us think of the latter, just as the inscription "balls" (or the associated sound) automatically makes us think of balls. We cannot read or hear a familiar name without thinking of what it names. Yet "ball" is no more like balls than is "cube".

*If* there is no resemblance between visible shapes and tangible shapes, Berkeley has explained why we all overlook this fact. If; but it is a gratuitous paradox to claim that there is no resemblance. Berkeley supports this claim by arguing for a conclusion which was merely asserted by Locke: that if a congenitally blind man had learned by touch to distinguish a sphere and a cube, and he were 'made to see', he could not, by looking at them, and before he had touched them, tell which was which. Before arguing for this conclusion, Berkeley had argued that a man born blind could not, on first acquiring vision, recognize visible objects as more or less distant, or as more or less large, or as higher or lower; that he would have to learn what, for him, would be entirely new and arbitrary applications of *all* words for so-called primary qualities. Whether Berkeley and Locke were correct has been debated ever since by psychologists and philosophers. One might have hoped that the issue would by now have been settled by experiment, for there are about sixty recorded cases of the kind envisaged.[5] But Berkeley so describes his desired experiment that it is impracticable. It concerns 'the first act of vision', the blind man having gained his sight 'on a sudden'. But it takes some time for the patient to recover from the operation, and he cannot focus his eyes till a few days after the bandages are removed. So before he is ready to be experimented on, he will have had opportunities to do some learning.

Consider one of Berkeley's arguments concerning a man seeing for the first time:

> whatever object intercepts the view of another [object], hath an equal number of visible points . . . consequently they [the two objects] shall both be thought by him to have the same magnitude. Hence it is evident [that he] would judge his thumb, with which he might hide a tower, . . . equal to that tower (LXXIX).

But even while the patient's vision is still blurred, he will doubtless have looked in the direction of his hands, and noticed that, whenever he moves a hand towards (or away from) his head, something gets visibly larger (or smaller), and he may well have identified this visible something with his felt hand. But even if Berkeley's imaginary experiment were practicable and a man born blind could, in his first act of vision, focus clearly on a cube, what on earth could he make of the perspectival distortion of all, or all but one, of its faces? In his earlier experience of handling cubes there had been nothing corresponding to visible changes in shape and size which accompany changes in direction and distance from his head. *Of course* he would have to learn about this feature peculiar to vision, and *of course* he would have to learn our convention of ascribing to a flat surface the shape it looks $_{(ph)}$ from in front.

For what it is worth, there is some evidence against the conclusions reached by Locke and Berkeley. R. L. Gregory, the psychologist, recently tried to carry out their desired experiments on an intelligent man who was enabled to see by corneal grafting.[6] He reports that the patient 'could recognize block capital letters, and numbers, by sight without any special training. This surprised us greatly. It turned out that he had been taught upper case, though not lower case, letters at the blind school.' However, this patient's feat was not his 'first act of vision'; and there is some evidence that people have to learn to judge the sizes of distant objects. Studies have been made of people who have always lived in dense forests and have never seen very distant objects. We are told: 'When they are taken out of their forest, and shown distant objects, they see these not as distant, but as small.'[7] But do we need experiments to establish whether a visible square is more similar to a tangible square than is a visible circle? Berkeley says that 'the visible square is fitter than the visible circle to represent the tangible square, *but ... not because it is liker ...*'; yet he adds, with obvious inconsistency, that 'the visible figures which shall be most proper to mark it, contain four distinct equal parts, corresponding to the four sides of a tangible square' (CXLII; my italics). Here, Berkeley describes the respect in which a visible square (seen from in front) and a tangible square *are alike*, and unlike both a visible and a tangible circle!

A Representative theory of vision does not require us to deny that there are resemblances between the spatial features of visual sense-data and the spatial properties of things which are detected by touch and locomotion. Provided that we remember that, for example, a match-box has a constant tactual shape and size when held and moved by one's hand, but that the corresponding visual sense-data vary systematically in their shapes and sizes. Presumably one reason for our convention of ascribing to a flat surface the visible shape which it looks$_{(ph)}$ from in front, is that only this visible shape has the geometrical properties which are detected by touch, e.g. each side being equal in length in Berkeley's example of a square surface. But we must not sweep under the carpet the chief paradox involved in a Representative theory of vision. This, in Berkeley's words, is that 'it must be acknowledged that we never feel and see one and the same object'. And this would apply even when one is seeing one's hand! Berkeley was obliged to embrace this paradox because he asserted that visible objects or ideas are never 'at a distance'. (And though he starts by speaking as if visual sense-data are flat, two-dimensional, he ends by seeming to deny even this. See CXXX and CLVIII.) But I too seem obliged to embrace Berkeley's chief paradox. My reason for proposing a Representative theory of vision is my conclusion that the colours that one sees are created by one's CNS. In that case, what we see must presumably be sense-data *qua* transitory entities which cannot *be* surfaces of physical objects. Can anything be said which would make this paradox acceptable? Let us try.

The constituents of my visual field which I describe as distinct sense-data will be whatever I single out as gestalts, and what I do, normally, single out are what I recognize as (as representing) physical objects. For example, I single out a variously coloured shape which I see *as* an apple, a type of sense-datum which, as I had learned before I could talk, is a pretty reliable sign of the presence of an object which has a familiar texture, flavour, and odour. I shall, unlike Berkeley, respect the phenomenological facts. It is not merely true that I *interpret* my visual sense-data *as* objects located in a three-dimensional space. What is *sense*-given, my visual field, *is* three-dimensional. My apple sense-datum is visibly bulgy, and it is at various field-of-view distances from many other sense-data, these distances being in the near–far as well as the up–down and right–left dimensions. Though the contents of my visual field are created by my CNS, still they do have spatial properties of the same kinds, and of the same structure, as those which are detected by moving about and touching things. At any rate this is true of the volume of my visual field which is well within the range of stereoscopic vision.

Here we must note that the range of stereoscopic vision is much greater than it is said to be in books by psychologists. R. L. Gregory, who has done some important experimental work on vision, has recently written: 'We are effectively one-eyed for distances greater than about twenty feet.'[8] He had just been stressing the importance for distance perception of slight differences between what is visible to one's two eyes. It is surprising that experimental psychologists should go on repeating this statement about the range of stereoscopic vision, a statement whose falsity is easily confirmed. (Are they all short-sighted?) My own simple experiment involved propping vertically a fishing rod (R) and viewing it visibly in line with a flagpole (P) about a mile away. I placed myself 300 feet from R, so that P was visibly behind R, though, when using both eyes, both R and P were still visible.* I then kept my head motionless, and shut each eye in turn. On shutting my right eye, P was seen distinctly to the left of R, and on shutting my left eye distinctly to its right. (See Figure 5.) Even for an immobile spectator, binocular vision can reveal the relative distances of things at (towards) which one is looking, at a range at least 15 times greater than the maximum alleged by psychologists. Moreover, we are not immobile, and parallax reveals the relative distances of things much more distant. Merely by using your neck muscles, you can make a tree half a mile away visibly slide sideways against a distant hillside. By using other muscles, things which are several miles away can be made so to slide. It is not only tactual perception which is an active process. Ascertaining by sight the three-dimensional shapes of things normally requires locomotion, and the same goes for seeing the distances of distant objects.†

Berkeley's version of a Representative theory of vision is absurd, because it is founded on the falsehood that all that we *see* (as distinct from *judge*) are two-dimensional patterns of colours. A Representative theory of vision does not seem to be *absurd* if it respects the phenomenological facts, notably: (i) that the visual sense-data which represent things located up to several miles away

* For brevity, I write "R" and "P" instead of "the R-sense-datum", etc., as I should do here.

† Disparity of the sense-data in binocular vision, and parallax, are not the only features of our visual sense-data on which depends our perception of distances. In chapter 6 of *The Perception of the Visual World* (New York and Cambridge, Mass., 1950), J. J. Gibson stressed the importance of what he called 'texture gradients'. I am, however, inclined to classify texture gradients as clues from which we have learned to make unconscious inferences à la Berkeley and Helmholtz.

are, under favourable conditions, visibly at more or less definite distances; (ii) that the sense-data which represent many of the things located well within the range of stereoscopic vision are visibly at determinate distances. Surely we may conclude that the spatial structure of the nearer region of one's visual field is isomorphic with that of the corresponding region of physical space. I say 'the nearer region'. How near? It would be idle to offer any simple, general answer to this question, for the range of our stereoscopic vision has no fixed or precise limit, e.g. 20 or 300 feet. The further away the things that one is looking at (towards), the less determinate become the three-dimensional shapes and the visible

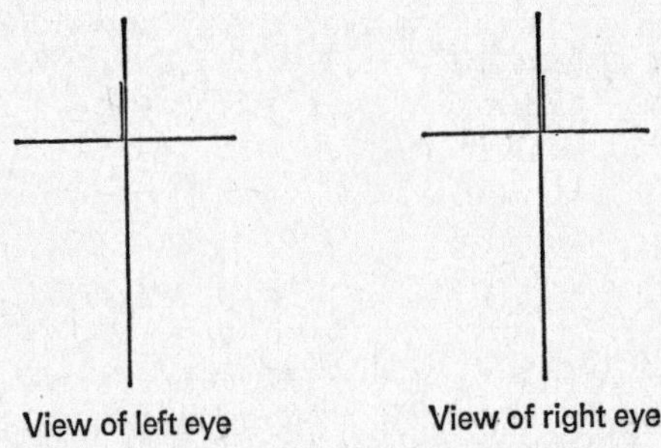


*Figure 5. Illustration of the disparity of the sense-data in binocular vision.* The short vertical lines represent the distant pole on the horizon, the long lines represent the nearer rod.

distances of the corresponding sense-data. Even in my simple experiment, the maximum range at which the rod and the pole are seen as depicted in Figure 5 will depend upon the thickness of both the rod and the pole, and on other conditions which it is for psychologists to investigate.

As we saw in chapter 4, a Representative theory of *perception* is self-defeating. Those who have embraced it seem to have done so primarily because they felt obliged to accept a Representative theory of *vision*, and forgot about their own bodies. A Representative theory of vision is not self-defeating if one is a Realist regarding proprio-perception and the spatio-temporal properties of physical things. We may be brusque in dismissing a Representative theory of proprio-perception. It is absurd to suppose that one is acquainted only with an 'image' of one's own body, a 'somatic sense-datum', and that one has to justify by inference (as if one then could) that one's body is not really coffin-shaped. I have outlined a non-homogeneous theory of perception which deserves, I think, to be considered seriously. Yet I must confess that I find it hard to believe when not in my study, and am reluctant to accept this theory.

Hume abandoned his attempt to solve the problems concerning perception, because he considered that there is a contradiction between 'our senses' and 'our reason'; namely that we cannot help believing that physical things exist when they are not being perceived and that they then continue to have sensible qualities, but that reason reveals that these beliefs cannot be true. My reasoning has not revealed any grounds for denying that physical things exist when not perceived, nor that they then lose their so-called primary qualities, nor that *external* things then cease to have secondary qualities in the only sense, a causal sense, in which they have them when they are perceived. But for me too there is a conflict between reason and 'the senses'; since I have concluded that colour-qualities, like sound-qualities, do not inhere in any body, unlike the sensible qualities peculiar to touch, taste, and smell which inhere, from time to time, in *our* bodies. Yet colours, unlike the so-called primary qualities, are qualities, and must presumably be qualities *of* something; and so I seem obliged to ascribe them to sense-data *qua* transitory by-products of the CNS.

The arguments which have led me to this conclusion do, however, leave open one alternative to that of adopting a Representative theory of vision; namely the theory of which Broad has written: 'If this be not nonsense, I do not know what nonsense is.' This alternative is to adopt Realism regarding the things that we see and their spatial properties, but not about colour-qualities; to maintain that when I look at a penny, what I see, the so-called sense-datum, *is* the front surface of the penny, that the sense-given shape and size (if there is no distorting medium) is the *penny*'s shape and size *from here*, but that the colour that I see is 'projected' on to that external surface. Broad makes this thesis sound nonsensical by saying: 'We are asked to believe that there is brownness without shape "in me", and round shape without colour out there.' But need we say anything so odd? We do not say such things in cases where it is clear the colours that a person sees *on* an external surface *must* be generated by his CNS; e.g. when one sees after-image colours on grey paper, or sees green and magenta shadows cast on white paper by two yellow lamps. If you ask *where* such colours are, what can this mean but 'where are they seen?' Broad's phrase "brownness without shape in me" is a by-product of taking literally his metaphorical use of "projected". The thought is that just as the transparency must exist in the projector before it can be thrown on to the screen, so the brownness must exist in my mind before it can be thrown on to the penny. But we need not be misled by our metaphors. The view that colours are created by the CNS need not be construed as implying that colours exist 'in the mind'. Whether we shall want to say this will depend on our solution to a family of problems not dealt with in this book—'the mind–body problem'. I am tempted to accept the position which Broad deemed a paradigm case of nonsense. Then what is it that is visibly red when I look at a tomato? (I complained earlier that Smart had not answered this question.) I shall have to say that "something is visibly red" means only that something, the tomato, now $looks_{(ph)}$ red, and deny that this (or any other) colour is an inherent property of this (or any other) physical object, if by "an inherent property of M" is meant a property which M has independently of its being seen, a property which physical objects had before evolution produced organisms with eyes like ours. The thesis that colour qualities are, in this sense, inherent properties of physical objects should, I think, be called '*Naïve* Realism'. And if its exponents neglect the relevant phenomenological facts and base their case on issuing reminders about English grammar, I suggest that this procedure scarcely deserves to be called philosophy.

My conclusions are not offered as accounts of how we talk in English, American, or any other natural languages, nor of what 'we' (average English, etc., speakers) mean by our everyday utterances; but rather as what we seem to be obliged to say if we have surveyed and reflected critically about all the relevant empirical facts. If my conclusions about sensible qualities other than colours are so interpreted, I do not think they should be found hard to accept. I cannot say the same about my rejection of Realism concerning colours. I find this hard to swallow and wish it were avoidable. It is hard to believe when one is using one's eyes and not merely thinking about their use. I have a well-nigh irresistible urge to ascribe colours to physical things. So I end, like Hume, with a conflict between reason and *one* of my senses, a conflict whose scope is fortunately much more limited than Hume's. To forget this conflict, I do not need to play backgammon or remind myself about English usage. All I need do is look at things and drink in the colours which I cannot but see as *theirs*. Yet when, again, I think about vision, I cannot believe that physical things have colours in the sense in which they have shapes.

The respect in which my verdict is most tentative is that I hesitate between the alternative accounts of vision which I have outlined in this chapter. The first is a Representative theory of vision. The second, merely adumbrated and not yet explored, seeks to combine a Realist theory of *vision* with a Representative theory of *colour*. I apologize to reviewers for offering an account of perception which cannot be given a simple label. I hope, however, that despite my accepting a Representative theory regarding the ascription to *external* things of what *I* call 'sensible qualities', my claim to be defending a Realist theory of perception will not be disputed. The first of the alternative conclusions between which I hesitate involves rejecting only one of the tenets in terms of which I have defined "Realism", the one concerning the 'immediacy' of vision, and the other alternative involves accepting all eight of these tenets. If anyone denies that my position may be called 'Realism', I suggest that he starts by explaining how he defines "Realism" in this context.

## Postscript

I now think that the hybrid theory of vision outlined on pages 178–9 above will have to be abandoned in favour of a Representative theory of vision. My preoccupation with colour vision had led me to neglect some of the factors which may affect the phenomenal shapes, etc. of things seen. The argument which I used on pages 146–7 will commit me to a Representative theory of vision *if* changes in the shapes, sizes or relative directions of a person's visual sense-data are dependent on the states of his CNS. And there is some evidence indicating that this is so. Anyone who wishes to defend the hybrid theory of vision should consider whether it can be reconciled with the facts described by Gregory in *Eye and Brain*, chapters 9 and 11 and especially pages 204–14.

# Numbered References

*Introduction*

1. *A Treatise of Human Nature* (1739), I. IV. II, ed. D. G. C. MacNabb, London and Glasgow, 1962.

*Chapter 1*

1. *Sense and Sensibilia,* Oxford, 1962, pp. 90–1.
2. Reported in the *British Journal of Psychology,* 1930–1, pp. 339–67; 1931–2, pp. 1–30; 1931–2, pp. 216–41.
3. Op. cit., 1930–1, pp. 351–5.
4. *Sense and Sensibilia,* section II.
5. *A Discourse on Method* (1637), Part IV, and *Meditations on the First Philosophy* (1641), I. Both are included in *Descartes, A Discourse on Method, etc.,* Everyman's Library, London and New York, 1912.
6. *Some Main Problems of Philosophy,* London and New York, 1953, II.
7. Op. cit., 1931–2, p. 23.
8. Op. cit., 1931–2, p. 222.
9. Op. cit., 1931–2, pp. 229–34.
10. Op. cit., 1930–1, pp. 347–8.
11. *Eye and Brain,* London, 1966, pp. 152–3.

*Chapter 2*

1. *Perception,* London, 1932, p. 35.
3. Price, *Perception,* ch. II; Ayer, *The Foundations of Empirical knowledge,* London, 1940, ch. I.
3. *Sense and Sensibilia,* p. 92.
4. *The Problems of Perception,* London and New York, 1959, p. 49.
5. See Gregory, *Eye and Brain,* pp. 212–13.

6. *Language, Truth and Logic* (1936); page-references in this book refer to the revision edition, London, 1946, here pp. 57–9.
7. *Analysis of Perception*, London, 1956, pp. 85–91.
8. Society for Psychical Research, *Proceedings*, 1894. See also ch. IV of C. D. Broad's *Lectures on Psychical Research*, London, 1962.
9. For details see S.P.R., *Proceedings*, 1920, pp. 152ff.
10. *The Nature of Hypnosis*, ed. R. E. Shor and M. T. Orne, London, 1965, pp. 89ff.

*Chapter 3*

1. In his introduction to the Fontana edition of Locke's *Essay*, London, 1964.
2. *Of the Principles of Human Knowledge* (1710), XIV and XV, contained in *Berkeley, New Theory of Vision, etc.*, Everyman's Library, London and New York, 1910.
3. Quoted by E. A. Burtt in *The Metaphysical Foundations of Modern Science*, London, 1932, p. 75.
4. See Burtt, op. cit., pp. 173–8.
5. *The Problems of Perception*, pp. 65–6.
6. W. Penfield and A. T. Rasmussen, *The Cerebral Cortex of Man*, New York, 1950; W. Penfield and L. Roberts, *Speech and Brain Mechanism*, Princeton, N.J., 1959. My quotations are from the latter.
7. *The Metaphysical Foundations of Modern Science*, p. 266.
8. *Mathematical Principles*, a revised translation by Florian Cajori of Newton's *Principia* (1687), Cambridge, 1934, p. 398.
9. *Opera*, London, 1779–85, vol. IV, p. 305.
10. Pp. 124–5 in the 1952 edition by Dover Publications Ltd.
11. Query 13 in *Optiks*, pp. 345–6 in 1952 edition.
12. W. A. H. Rushton, 'Visual Pigments in Man', *Scientific American*, Nov. 1962.
13. W. B. Marks, W. H. Dobelle, and E. F. MacNichol, 'Visual Pigments of Single Primate Cones', *Science*, 1964, pp. 1181–2; E. F. MacNichol, 'Three Pigment Color Vision', *Scientific American*, Dec. 1964. (Separate reprints of *Scientific American* articles are usually available.)
14. See G. Wyszecki and W. S. Stiles, *Color Science*, New York, 1967, pp. 413, 582–7.
15. See the papers on colour vision in fish and animals in the CIBA Foundation Symposium, *Colour Vision*, London, 1965.
16. See G. M. Wyburn *et al.*, *Human Senses and Perception*, Edinburgh and London, 1964, ch. 1.
17. *The Nature of the Physical World*, London, 1928, p. xiii.

*Chapter 4*

1. A. D. Woozley, introduction to Locke's *Essay*, Fontana Library edition, p. 27.
2. For example, by H. H. Price in *Perception*, ch. IV.
3. *Perception*, p. 92.
4. See his *Second Dialogue* in the Everyman volume, *Berkeley, New Theory of Vision, etc.*
5. *Language, Truth and Logic*, p. 35.
6. Ibid., p. 53.
7. Ibid., p. 64.

*Chapter 5*

1. *Berkeley*, Harmondsworth, 1969, pp. 147–8.
2. At the top of p. 216 in the Everyman volume, *Berkeley, New Theory of Vision, etc.*
3. See also Ayer, *The Foundations of Empirical Knowledge*, pp. 263–74.
4. *The Problems of Philosophy*, OPUS Edition, London, 1967, pp. 13–14.
5. 'The Argument from Illusion', in *Contemporary British Philosophy*, ed. H. D. Lewis, London, 1956, vol. III.
6. *Berkeley*, pp. 147–8.
7. See J. P. Sutcliffe's papers on '"Credulous" and "Skeptical" Views about Hypnotic Phenomena', in *The Nature of Hypnosis*, ed. Shor and Orne.

*Chapter 6*

1. *The Mind and its Place in Nature*, London, 1925, pp. 200ff.
2. *Perception*, ch. 2.
3. *The Problems of Perception*, pp. 76–8.
4. *Philosophy and the Physicists*, London, 1937, pp. 51–3.
5. Ibid., p. 60.
6. *The Concept of Mind*, London, 1949, p. 220.
7. See his *Philosophy and Scientific Realism*, London and New York, 1963, esp. chs. II and IV.
8. *New Systems of Chemical Philosophy*, London, 1808.
9. *Philosophy and Scientific Realism*, p. 39.
10. *An Inquiry into Meaning and Truth*, London, 1940, p. 15.

*Chapter 7*

1. 'Is there a Problem about Sense-data?' *Proc. Arist. Soc.*, suppl. vol., 1936.
2. 'On the So-called Space of Sight', *Proc. Arist. Soc.*, 1927–8, p. 97.
3. *The Problem of Knowledge*, London and New York, 1956, pp. 122–3.

4. See, for example, Ayer's papers 2 and 3 in *The Concept of a Person*, London, 1963.
5. *The Foundations of Empirical Knowledge*, p. 135; cf. pp. 116–17.
6. Ibid., p. 83.
7. *Scientific Thought*, London, 1923, p. 244.
8. See his review of *The Foundations of Empirical Knowledge* in *Mind*, 1941, pp. 286–8.
9. *The Mind and its Place in Nature*, pp. 410–15.
10. 'The Problem of Perception', *Mind*, 1955, pp. 38–9.
11. See *Sense and Sensibilia*, ch. IV.
12. 'Has Austin Refuted the Sense-Datum Theory?' *Synthese*, vol. 17, 1967.
13. See *The Foundations of Empirical Knowledge*, p. 80.

*Chapter 8*

1. See the report of its Committee on Colorimetry, *Journ. Opt. Soc. of Amer.*, 1943, and Ralph M. Evans, *An Introduction to Color*, New York and London, 1948, ch. 1.
2. *Berkeley*, p. 148.
3. Ibid., p. 148.
4. 'Seeming', *Proc. Arist. Soc.*, suppl. vol., 1952, p. 246.
5. *Perception and our Knowledge of the External World*, London, 1967, p. 100.
6. See W. D. Wright, *Researches on Normal and Defective Colour Vision*, London, 1946; The Committee on Colorimetry, *The Science of Color*, New York, 1953, pp. 134–44.
7. *An Introduction to Color*, pp. 196–7.
8. *The Concept of Prayer*, London, 1965, pp. 50–1.

*Chapter 9*

1. *Principia Ethica*, Cambridge, 1903, ch. 1.
2. Evans, *An Introduction to Color*, p. 230.
3. See Colour Plates 11 to 17 in the Committee on Colorimetry, *The Science of Color*.
4. H. von Helmholtz, *Physiological Optics*, vol. 2, pp. 285ff. in 1924 edition published by the Optical Society of America.
5. Hans Wallach, 'The Perception of Neutral Colors', *Scientific American*, January 1963.
6. Harry Helson and V. B. Jeffers, 'Fundamental Problems in Color Vision II', *Journ. Exper. Psych.*, 1940, p. 13.
7. Harry Helson, 'Fundamental Problems in Color Vision I', *Journ. Exp. Psych.*, 1938, p. 468.
8. Evans, *An Introduction to Color*, p. 131.

9. 'Experiments in Color Vision', *Scientific American*, May 1959; reprinted in R. C. Teevan and R. C. Birney (eds.), *Color Vision*, Princeton, N.J., Toronto, and London, 1961.
10. See W. A. H. Rushton's paper 'The Eye, the Brain and Land's Two-Colour Projections', in *Nature*, 1961, pp. 440–2.
11. 'Appraisal of Land's Work on Two-Primary Color Projection', *Journ. Opt. Soc. Amer.*, March, 1960.
12. Helson, 'Fundamental Problems in Color Vision I'; Helson and Jeffers, 'Fundamental Problems in Color Vision II'; Deane B. Judd, 'Hue Saturation and Lightness of Surface Colors with Chromatic Illumination', *Journ. Opt. Soc. Amer.*, 1940.
13. Helson and Jeffers, op. cit., p. 7.
14. 'Some Factors and Implications of Color Constancy', *Journ. Opt. Soc. Amer.*, 1943, p. 564.
15. *Scientific Thought*, pp. 273–4.

*Chapter 10*

1. Austin, *Sense and Sensibilia*, p. 114.
2. *Philosophical Papers*, Oxford, 1961, p. 123.
3. *Proc. Arist. Soc.*, suppl. vol. 1952, p. 241.
4. *Proc. Arist. Soc.*, suppl. vol., 1954, p. 81.
5. Moore's 'An Autobiography' in *The Philosophy of G. E. Moore*, ed. P. Schilpp, La Salle, Ill., 1942, p. 14.
6. *Language, Truth and Logic*, pp. 57, 59.
7. Schilpp, ed. cit., p. 362.
8. *English Philosophy Since 1900*, Oxford, 1958, p. 167.
9. *Contemporary Moral Philosophy*, London, 1967, pp. 1–2, and his Introduction to *The Philosophy of Perception*, Oxford, 1967.
10. *Philosophical Papers*, p. 130.
11. *Sense and Sensibilia*, pp. 62–3.
12. *The Concept of a Person*, p. 20.
13. *Tractatus Logico-Philosophicus*, Oxford, 1922, 4.0031.
14. See, for example, C. A. Mace's paper in *Proc. Arist. Soc.*, 1948–9, pp. 1–16.
15. *Language, Truth and Logic*, p. 129.
16. *Philosophy and Scientific Realism*, pp. 78–84.
17. *Principles of Empirical Realism*, Springfield, Ill., 1966, pp. 175, 228–9.

*Chapter 11*

1. *Leviathan*, Introduction.
2. See pp. 84–5, above.
3. See J. J. Gibson, *The Senses Considered as Perceptual Systems*, Boston, Mass., 1968, chs. VI and VII.

4. *Perception and Our Knowledge of the External World,* London and New York, 1967.
5. M. von Senden, *Space and Sight,* transl. P. L. Heath, New York, 1960.
6. *Eye and Brain,* pp. 193–8.
7. Ibid., pp. 161–2.
8. Ibid., p. 53.

# Recommended Reading for Students

Anyone anxious to be persuaded that philosophers' problems about perception are, after all, bogus need read only the last book on my list, and should refrain from reading the books criticized therein. Others are advised to read some classical texts before embarking on recent philosophy and to acquaint themselves at an early stage with some of the relevant science.

*Scientific Background*

As an introduction I recommend the following books, which are arranged roughly in the order in which I think they will be found readable by Arts students.

LOCKLEY, R. M.: *Animal Navigation*, London, 1967.

GREGORY, R. L.: *Eye and Brain*, London, 1966.

WYBURN, G. M., PICKFORD, R. W., and HIRST, R. J.: *Human Senses and Perception*, Edinburgh and London, 1964, Parts I (on Physiology) and II (on Psychology).

DAMPIER-WHETHAM, W. C. DAMPIER: *A History of Science*, Cambridge, 1929, chapters III and IV.

BURTT, E. A.: *The Metaphysical Foundations of Modern Science*, revised edition, London, 1932.

BORING, E. G.: *Sensation and Perception in the History of Experimental Psychology*, New York, 1942.

GIBSON, J. J.: *The Perception of the Visual World*, New York and Cambridge, Mass., 1950.

GIBSON, J. J.: *The Senses Considered as Perceptual Systems*, London, 1968.

TEEVAN, R. C., and BIRNEY, R. C. (eds.): *Color Vision*, Princeton, N.J., Toronto, and London, 1961.

EVANS, RALPH M.: *An Introduction to Color*, New York and London, 1948.

NEWTON, ISAAC: *Optiks* (1704), New York, 1962.

HELMHOLTZ, H. VON: *Treatise on Physiological Optics* (1886), ed. James P. C. Southall, New York, 1962, vols. II and III.

COMMITTEE ON COLORIMETRY OF OPTICAL SOCIETY OF AMERICA: *The Science of Color*, New York, 1953.

(*Note*: At the time of writing, there is no comprehensive and readable book which is up to date on developments in the science of colour vision.)

*Philosophy*

The works recommended below are arranged in the order in which they were written (with a few exceptions among the more recent books). I recommend that they be read in this order. Philosophers' theories have usually been developed via criticism of their predecessors' theories. The connections between philosophers' problems are more easily grasped if the river of time is followed downstream.

DESCARTES, RENÉ: *Meditations on the First Philosophy* (1641). Included in *Descartes, A Discourse on Method, etc.*, Everyman's Library, London and New York, 1912.

LOCKE, JOHN: *An Essay Concerning Human Understanding* (1690), Books I and II, esp. chapters VIII, IX, and XXIII of Book II. Available in Everyman's Library, ed. J. W. Yolton, London and New York, 1961, and Fontana Library, ed. A. D. Woozley, London and Glasgow, 1964.

BERKELEY, GEORGE: *An Essay Towards a New Theory of Vision* (1709).

BERKELEY, GEORGE: *Of the Principles of Human Knowledge* (1710).

BERKELEY, GEORGE: *Three Dialogues* (1713).

All are contained in *Berkeley, New Theory or Vision, etc.*, Everyman's Library, London and New York, 1910.

HUME, DAVID: *A Treatise of Human Nature* (1739), Book I, esp. Part IV. Available in Everyman's Library, ed. A. D. Lindsay, London and New York, 1911, and Fontana Library, ed. D. G. C. MacNabb, London, 1962.

REID, THOMAS: *Essays on the Intellectual Powers of Man* (1785), ed. A. D. Woozley, London, 1941, Essays I, II, and VI.

MILL, JOHN STUART: 'Berkeley's Life and Writing' (1871). Available in *Dissertations and Discussions*, London, 1875, vol. IV.

RUSSELL, BERTRAND: *The Problems of Philosophy* (1912), OPUS edition, London, 1967, chapters 1–5.

RUSSELL, BERTRAND: *Mysticism and Logic*, London, 1917, chapters VII and VIII.

RUSSELL, BERTRAND: *Analysis of Matter*, London and New York, 1927, Part II.

MOORE, G. E.: *Some Main Problems of Philosophy*, London and New York, 1953 (but these lectures were given forty years earlier), chapters II and VII.

MOORE, G. E.: *Philosophical Papers*, London and New York, 1959 (but these papers were published earlier), Essays II and VII.

BROAD, C. D.: *Scientific Thought*, London, 1923, Part II, chapters VII and VIII.

PRICE, H. H.: *Perception*, London, 1932, esp. chapters I, II, IV, V, and VIII.

PRICE, H. H.: *Hume's Theory of the External World*, Oxford, 1940, esp. chapters I–IV.

AYER, A. J.: *The Foundations of Empirical Knowledge*, London, 1940, esp. chapters I, II, and V.

AYER, A. J.: *The Problem of Knowledge*, London and New York, 1956, chapter III.

WARNOCK, G. J.: *Berkeley* (1953), re-issued with new Preface, Harmondsworth, 1969.

HIRST, R. J.: *The Problems of Perception*, London and New York, 1959, chapters I–VI.

SMART, J. J. C.: *Philosophy and Scientific Realism*, London and New York, 1963, esp. chapters II and IV.

LOCKE, DON: *Perception and our Knowledge of the External World*, London and New York, 1967.

AUSTIN, J. L.: *Sense and Sensibilia*, Oxford, 1962.

# Index